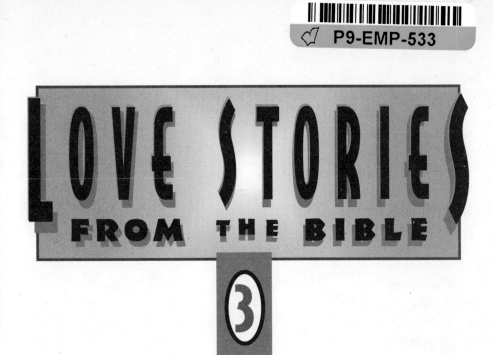

LOVE STORIES FROM THE BIBLE

3

Additional materials have been prepared by:
Word Searches: Bob Coffen
Puzzles: Beverly Kelly
"A Closer Look": Gerald Wheeler

Special Biblical and Archaeological Consultants
>   Douglas Clark
>   Larry Herr
>   Siegfried Horn
>   Sakae Kubo
>   Pedrito Maynard-Reid
>   Ron Springett
>   Warren Trenchard

Bible stories by Ruth Redding Brand
Professor Appleby narrative by Charles Mills

Professor Appleby and the Maggie B Tapes Series
1. *Mysterious Stories From the Bible*
2. *Amazing Stories From the Bible*
3. *Love Stories From the Bible*

LOVE STORIES
FROM THE BIBLE
3

RUTH REDDING BRAND
& CHARLES MILLS

REVIEW AND HERALD® PUBLISHING ASSOCIATION
HAGERSTOWN, MD 21740

This book was
Edited by Gerald Wheeler
Designed by Patricia S. Wegh
Cover design by Ron J. Pride
Cover illustration by Kim Justinen
Interior illustrations by Joe Van Severen
Typeset: 12/14 Stone Informal

PRINTED IN U.S.A.

99 98 97 96 95   10 9 8 7 6 5 4 3 2 1

R&H Cataloging Service
Brand, Ruth Redding
   Love stories from the Bible, by Ruth
Redding Brand and Charles Mills.

   1. Bible stories. I. Mills, Charles
Henning, 1950- II. Title. III. Series.
            220.9505

ISBN 0-8280-0934-1

① The Darkness

I can't see a thing!" 10-year-old Stacey breathed, her hand motionless in front of her face. At least she *thought* her hand was there. It felt like it was, anyway.

"Everything looks the same whether my eyes are open or closed," someone added. The soft Mexican accent belonged to her best friend and classmate, Maria. "Are you sure it was like this before He spoke?" the girl queried.

Another youngster interjected, "It's so dark in here we're all invisible!"

A loud, long laugh erupted into the darkness. The deep male chortle often echoed down the endless hallways and high-ceiling rooms of the big mansion at the edge of the forest. Jason, the boy who'd just spoken, jumped at the sound, but then joined in. No need to be afraid. No need to run away from the happy laugh bursting from the mysterious gloom. Not when the sound came from Professor Appleby.

Even in the pitch-black room, the children recognized the sheer joy of their old friend sitting cross-legged on the floor next to them. "Wouldn't it be fun to be invisible in the light?" he said.

Then the children heard their friend draw in a deep breath and explode in another round of laughter. By now they couldn't help adding their own giggles. When Professor Appleby thought something was funny, *everyone* shared in his glee.

Stacey sat in the darkness, smiling broadly. How many kids had a grandfather like the professor? How many of her friends could boast such a strange and wonderful man as a member of their family? Not many, she was sure.

Her grandfather was one of a kind. The fact that he lived in an old Victorian mansion covered with ancient vines, set in a cleared spot surrounded by a forest of ageless oaks and elms near the river flowing along the edge of town, added to the mystery of the man.

Classmates at school thought he was just a little crazy in the head. Well, maybe he was. But if Professor Appleby could be considered crazy, then Stacey felt the world needed to be filled with such old men with hearts and smiles like his.

"Grandfather?" she called into the inky darkness. "Aren't you forgetting something?"

The old man's laughter slowly died to an occasional chuckle. "What did you say?" he asked.

"Aren't you forgetting something?" Stacey repeated.

"I don't think so," the unseen professor replied.

"The tapes," the invisible Jason giggled. "That's why we're sitting in this dark room."

"Yeah," Maria added, "you wanted us to see what the world looked like before God began Creation Week."

"Tapes? What tapes?"

Stacey sighed a happy sigh. "The ones sent by Maggie B! Your sister. My great-aunt. She travels all over the world digging up old cities and sending you some of the stuff she finds."

"Oh yes, Maggie B," the old man said warmly. "She's such a nice person. But I do miss her. Why, if it weren't for those tapes . . . *The tapes!*" the children heard their friend gasp. Then he quickly added, "Bet you think that I've forgotten that's why we're sitting here in the middle of my den with all the lights off and the curtains tightly drawn." He began to laugh even more uproariously.

Stacey sighed and shook her head even though no one could see her in the darkness. "So we'd better get started," she urged with a laugh.

"Now, let me see," she and the others heard her grandfather mumble as the clattering noise of someone rummaging through a box of cassettes drifted in from nearby. "Which one is it? Hard to tell. Can't see a thing. Wait. Maybe it's this one."

1

The unmistakable sound of a tape being slipped noisily into a waiting player broke the silence. "There, that should do it. I'll press the play button and—"

Suddenly the room filled with a high-pitched female voice warbling the aria to some Italian opera. Professor Appleby quickly silenced it.

"Wrong tape," the old man announced. Another cassette slipped unseen into the machine, and a button clicked.

"I left my dog when I headed for the city with five bucks in my jeans." A male singer with a pronounced southern drawl belted out the words accompanied by a twanging guitar.

Click! "Nope. Wrong again. That's country music. I don't even like country music. How'd that get in there?"

Stacey and the other children suppressed their giggles as yet another tape clattered into the machine.

This time, a familiar voice echoed through the dark room. No mistaking Maggie B's energy and enthusiasm. There, in the pitch-black emptiness, a story began.

⚔ ⚔ ⚔ ⚔

Where is the darkest place you have ever been? Perhaps it was your home when the lights went out because of a storm. On a moonless night, before anyone found the candles or a flashlight, it was dark, wasn't it? Now think about the darkest place you can even imagine. How about the bottom of a coal mine at midnight, with someone holding black velvet-gloved hands over your eyes?

Before God made this world, it was even darker than that.

Now, what is the most water you have ever seen? A broad river? A lake? An ocean that never seems to end? But every river has another side. Lakes have their shorelines, and even the vast oceans wash up thousands of miles away on sandy beaches and rocky shores.

Before God made our world, water covered everything. A shoreless black ocean rolled around a coal-black planet. Nothing more.

Then God stepped into the blackness and the nothingness, and He spoke. At the sound of His voice, dazzling light drove back the darkness, lit up endless space, and shone on the spinning planet we call earth.

The next day God spoke again, and blue sky with its life-giving oxygen swept through the waters and divided them. Wrapping around the spinning planet like a soft blanket, the atmosphere forced the water vapor upward from the endless ocean.

Then up through the water and through shining mists mountains pushed their peaks, and on the third day valleys stretched themselves before their Creator. At His command the mountains and valleys shone with a living green. Enormous trees sprang into being, and flowers suddenly danced in the valleys and raced up the mountainsides.

On the fourth day the Creator spoke and the empty sky blazed with an enormous ball we know as the sun and a smaller shining ball we call the moon. As darkness fell, stars scattered across the endless stretches of night sky.

At the voice of God the mists vanished, and lakes, ponds, rivers, and seas shimmered in the sunshine. On the fifth day silvery fish and sea creatures appeared at God's command, churning the water as they swam and played. Another word, and mockingbirds and hummingbirds, eagles and toucans, birds of all descriptions, filled the air with music and color and the whisper of their wings.

The next day in a vacant valley a flock of sheep suddenly grazed while frogs croaked from a nearby pond and elephants trumpeted a triumphant note. On the mountaintops, goats leaped and climbed, while lions and leopards, cows and cats, dogs, deer, rabbits, and a thousand other animals frolicked in the wonderful new world.

God looked around and smiled. But He had not finished yet. The world was beautiful. Everything in it was perfect, but He hadn't created it for Himself. He had in mind a wonderful creature, a creature that would be very much like Himself. But God did not speak this creature into existence. Kneeling on the ground, He scraped up the soil, shaping it with strong fingers.

Carefully, lovingly, He worked. He pulled the claylike soil and stretched it. His fingertips pinched a little here, shaped more carefully there. At last a human form lay on the ground—a body with perfectly shaped arms, legs, and toes. It had broad shoulders and a finely shaped head. As though asleep, it lay in the dust like a life-sized doll.

Then God bent over the quiet face and breathed ever so gently into the mouth of the newly formed creature. Its eyelids fluttered. The creature opened his eyes and stood upright. It was tall. It was handsome. It was man.

Gently God smiled at His human creation. "Welcome to Eden," He said.

God called the man Adam. Adam looked in wonder around him. A brand-new being in a brand-new world, his heart beat with love for the God who had created him and this green, life-filled planet.

Taking Adam's hand, God showed him a special place on Planet Earth that He had created especially for him. It was breathtakingly beautiful, a garden park in which the man would make his home. Then, as the curious animals passed before him, Adam's quick mind named them one after another. He chuckled at the monkeys and smiled at the long neck of a giraffe. With pleasure he ran his fingers through the thick mane of a lion. But after seeing all the animals, Adam suddenly felt lonely. All the animals had mates, but he had none.

Then God put Adam into a deep sleep. From Adam's side God removed one rib. Taking the rib, He carefully built another creature. It was like Adam, yet different too, for the lines of its body were softer and more graceful. The shoulders were not as broad, nor was it as tall. Its face was as handsome as Adam's, but more delicate. God smiled as He gently woke Adam and presented him with this beautiful

surprise, the last and loveliest of all creation. The beautiful creature was a woman.

Adam's joy was boundless. The first man and the first woman loved each other. They became husband and wife, Adam and Eve.

The seventh day of Creation dawned, fresh and beautiful. Still smiling at Adam and Eve, God proclaimed, "This seventh day of Creation week is holy. Today I will rest from work and stay especially close to you."

Adam and Eve sat at the feet of their Creator, marveling at the animals, from the tiny ant to the huge mastodon. They breathed deeply of the flower-scented air and feasted their eyes on the green carpet of grass, rushing waterfalls, and brightly painted orchids.

Then they gazed into the face of their Creator. They had never seen Planet Earth when it had been a black and lifeless ball in space, but somehow they knew that God was a worker of miracles, and they bowed and worshiped Him.

And God, looking into Adam's and Eve's shining eyes, laughed a low, happy laugh. These two beautiful, brand-new people loved His creation. And they loved Him.

✕ ✕ ✕ ✕

The voice on the tape faded as the machine clicked to a stop. Stacey and the others sat in the darkness, thinking about what they'd just heard.

"It must have been beautiful," Maria sighed. "I wish I could've seen it."

"The earth hadn't been hurt by sin yet," Professor Appleby added. "There was nothing to mess up the Creator's handiwork."

"Yeah, you were right," Jason interjected. "Adam and Eve were lucky. When God made the world, they didn't have to pull weeds or worry about getting stung by a stink bug."

"A what?" Stacey giggled.

"A stink bug. That's what my mom calls 'em. They come

out every summer. Don't know what their real name is."

"Lots of bugs bite," they heard the professor announce in the darkness. "They're just trying to defend their territories." He paused. "That's what sin brought into this world—a bunch of people and animals trying to defend their territories."

"I'll bet the Creator knew all about stink bugs and birds and animals," Stacey pitched in. "After all, He created them." A moment later she added, "Hey, Grandfather?"

"Yes?"

"Do you think we can have the lights now? The world's been made. Adam and Eve had the sun in the daytime, and the moon and stars at night."

"You're right," the old man answered. Then he hesitated. "There's just one problem."

"What?"

"I don't think I'll be able to find the switch. I know it's over that way . . . or is it this way?"

Jason giggled. "Don't worry; I'll find it."

They heard the boy stumble to his feet. "Now, if I just head in this direction, I'll—" *CRASH!*

"What happened?" Professor Appleby gasped. "Are you all right?"

"I'm OK. But your coffee table might need a little touch up," the boy called from across the room. "Now there's something sticking in my nose, and I don't know what it is."

"In your nose?" Maria laughed.

Suddenly light bathed the room. Hands shot to eyes to shield them from the brilliance. Peeking between her fingers, Maria saw Stacey standing by the door, her thumb resting on the light switch, a smile spreading across her face. "I found it," she called.

As eyes adjusted to the illumination, Maria, Stacey, and Professor Appleby discovered Jason standing in one corner of the room surrounded by a large, green plant. In the darkness, he'd walked right into one of the professor's broad-leafed indoor shrubs. The boy's face was buried deep in the soft green foliage.

"Hey Jason," Maria called, "whatcha doin' in that big bush? Building a nest?"

Professor Appleby hurried over to his young friend and began helping the boy untangle himself from the branches. "Maybe we should change your name to Robin . . . you know . . . like the bird."

Stacey joined her grandfather. "Jason, you look a little bushed," she teased.

The boy pulled a leaf from his collar and smiled. "Remind me not to go wandering around in Professor Appleby's house with the lights off again. There's no tellin' where I'd end up."

Maria stretched stiff leg muscles. "Just be glad you didn't end up over there by the racks of clothes from the Middle East, the ones Maggie B sent. If you'd bumped into one of those and knocked them down on top of you, you might've ended up looking like the prince of Baghdad."

Stacey waved her hand in the air. "Wait a minute, Grandfather. You said you had three tapes for us today. How about playing the second one with the lights on so Jason won't get lost and we won't have to hear someone singing about leaving his dog?"

Professor Appleby nodded. "Let's head over by the couch, and I'll put the next cassette in the machine. It's a terrific story about what God did right after He made the world."

The group dropped to the floor and eagerly watched their old friend slip another tape into the player. Then, with contented sighs and smiles everyone could now see, they waited for the gentle voice of Maggie B to carry them to a long-ago time in a faraway place.

⚔ ⚔ ⚔ ⚔

Never has there been a party like the Creation Day celebration of Adam and Eve. First, Adam, newly alive, opened his eyes and looked into the face of God. Then God showed him his beautiful garden home.

Adam gazed around him, fascinated. Friendly animals paraded before him. Thousands of flowers—daisies, violets, and orchids—danced in the sunlight. Redwoods stretched to the sky, and robins warbled from their branches. A silvery river flowed through the center of the garden.

Then God gave Eve to Adam.

Now it was Eve's turn for surprises. She looked at God Himself and knew that He had made her. Then Eve gazed deeply into Adam's delighted eyes and smiled back her growing love for him.

"You are what I've been looking for," he told her. "You are a part of me, for you were made from my very bone."

Next God gave them a special gift—the gift of marriage. "Now," He said, "you are king and queen of this world. Take care of the plants and animals in this garden, for it is yours to enjoy."

Adam and Eve explored the garden. Holding hands, they splashed through a waterfall. Suddenly they stopped, startled by their reflections in the river, then laughed at the surprised looks on each other's face. They tried to count all the kinds of fruit that dangled from scores of trees, but decided it was much more fun simply to eat the fruit! Tenderly they touched the velvety petals of roses and lilies, and buried their noses in sweet-smelling honeysuckle. Stretching themselves on the soft carpet of deep, soft grass, they pillowed their heads on the warm roundness of a purring tiger. Through the branches of a maple they gazed at the bright blue sky.

As they talked the day away, something began to happen. The sky began to change from brilliant blue to pink, lavender, gold, and red. Adam and Eve hardly breathed. Constantly changing, the sky glowed with golden fire. It blazed with red glory, then beamed with pink and purple splendor. And the sun—the great golden sun—began to slip from the sky. Down, down it slid, and as it lowered, it became so red that it bathed the whole garden with a rosy glow.

Then they heard a voice, a wonderful voice they knew and loved. The Creator, more glorious than the glowing sky, stood before them. "What you see," He explained, "is a sunset. It marks the beginning of the seventh day of Creation. I am giving you the seventh day as a special present. On this day I will meet with you, and together we will remember Creation week. From sunset on the sixth day until sunset on the seventh day will be the Sabbath, a day of rest and celebration."

As the sun slid below the horizon and the stars came out, Adam and Eve and the Creator talked together. The couple had so many questions. Were they the only beings whom God had created besides the animals? God told them about angels. Where did God live? He explained about heaven. Why had God created this beautiful world when He already had a whole universe? Because they, Adam and Eve, were already in His mind, and He loved them.

"Tell us," they begged, "what You made first." So God told them what He had done on each day, explaining why He had created things in the order in which He did. Plants needed air and sunlight. Fish had to have water to swim in, and animals must have it to drink. The land had to be made so the grass could grow and the animals could eat. Adam's and Eve's eyes grew wide with wonder as they listened to God.

The next morning the golden sun climbed back into the sky, and every blade of grass, every shrub, leaf, and vine, sparkled with dew. And waiting for them in the garden was God.

Sabbath morning! Other than God's wonderful love itself, Adam and Eve knew that the Sabbath was the finest and best of all His gifts. It was His extra-special time with them. Suddenly they heard music. It was not the songs of the birds, the ripple of the river, nor the loud rumble of a lion. Sweet and glorious, it rose and fell, then swelled again in a harmony so beautiful that the listeners felt their hearts would burst. Thousands of voices blended in an anthem of praise to their Creator. Then Adam and Eve saw them— bright, shining beings, radiant with love and goodness, joyfully singing. Angels! Hardly knowing what they were doing, Adam and Eve opened their mouths and sang too. And God sang with them.

All day long Adam and Eve explored their brand new home with God. He led them to a mossy bank where a stream tumbled and gurgled over gold and silver stones. Rainbow trout swam to the bank at the sound of their Creator's voice.

"How do they breathe?" Adam asked.

God explained to him the secrets of the water and the secrets of the air. Together Adam and Eve learned about oxygen. Their Creator explained how their lungs and their blood systems worked.

Eve wanted to know about the stars. "Let's start with the

star nearest to you," God said. "That star is the sun." And He told her how the sun's rays traveled through space and how it was close enough to keep the earth just the right temperature—not too hot and not too cold.

Adam and Eve listened to all that God said. From their splendid Teacher they quickly absorbed great lessons in astronomy and mathematics. Soon they could trace the path of the earth around the sun and map the journeys of other stars and planets.

But they wanted to learn more and more. God smiled at their eagerness.

"Every Sabbath we shall meet together like this," He said softly. "And you have forever to learn new things!"

Then God led them to a hill all green and silver with softly swaying grasses. Sparkling steps led gently upward. Eagerly they climbed them. At the top of the hill they looked down on their garden home. Alive with color and movement and beauty, it shone like a giant jewel.

The first man and woman turned to their Creator. "Thank You for creating this beautiful present for us. We love You for all You have done!"

Then once more the sky began to flame with gold and red. And once more a symphony of angel voices filled the earth with praise. Adam and Eve, king and queen of the garden called Eden, knelt in love and worship before the King of all creation, the King of the universe.

✕ ✕ ✕ ✕

As the story ended, Jason lifted his hand. "Professor? Is that why people go to church each weekend, to remember the Sabbath God created on the seventh day?"

"I believe so," the old man replied. "No matter where Maggie B is, no matter what the weather or how tired she is, she always treats the Sabbath like it's something special, something important. She's told me many times, 'We may not be able to walk and talk with the Creator like Adam and Eve did, but we can take time to think about Him, and enjoy the wonders of His power.'

"Even when we were kids, Maggie B and I would spend each Sabbath afternoon wandering through the woods, or sitting down by the river. She'd tell me her dreams, and I'd tell her mine. Then we'd listen to the birds singing and watch the clouds drifting overhead and try to imagine what it would be like to sit down and talk with God."

The children were silent for a long moment. When Maria finally spoke, her words were quiet, thoughtful. "But what happened, Professor? What happened to the world? It's not beautiful and perfect like it was in the garden."

The old man sighed. "That's the saddest story in the Bible. Adam and Eve did something that changed everything."

He reached down and slipped another tape into the machine. "Why don't we let my sister explain. She made this recording in a camp near the Tigris and Euphrates rivers in far off Iraq.

"No one knows the exact spot where the Garden of Eden rested, but it could have been near where she was. Maggie B says there's certainly no garden there now—only hot, sandy desert. She said to stand in that desert, you can't help realizing the terrible changes Adam's and Eve's mistake brought to God's perfect creation."

"Listen to what she says."

※ ※ ※ ※

Days flowed into perfect days in the beautiful Garden of Eden. But God had once said something that continued to puzzle Adam and Eve. "Die—" The word had dropped like a strange, dark object into the sunlit garden. When God spoke of the tree of the knowledge of good and evil, He had said, "Don't eat from that tree, for the day that you do, you will surely die."

Adam and Eve tried their best to imagine what it meant to die. Their minds grasped God's words, but they could not picture death. So they decided simply to obey God and not worry about dying.

Another strange thing had intrigued the couple. They heard of the angel Lucifer, the "light bearer," who had rebelled against God. This once-honored being, beautiful and intelligent beyond all others, had convinced many other angels that God was unfair. Although God had been patient and loving with Lucifer and his rebels, they still had hardened their hearts and become more evil. Then God had had to banish them from heaven. Lucifer became Satan, an outlaw and outcast.

Now the outlaw band of angels had only one purpose—to persuade still others to rebel against God. They looked at Adam and Eve in their paradise home, and saw how happy they were. Angry and jealous, Satan determined to persuade Adam and Eve to disobey God, to sin.

One day Eve followed a trail of bright red flowers, picking them as she went. Suddenly she looked around her. Why, here she was in the center of the garden! There was the tree of life from which she and Adam ate daily. And there . . . there was that other tree, the tree of the knowledge of good and evil. Eve gazed at it thoughtfully. It was a beautiful tree with wide-spreading branches, rich green leaves, and fragrant fruit large and lovely and perfect. *I wonder why God told us not to eat it,* she thought to herself.

"Has God, indeed, told you not to eat it?" inquired an unfamiliar voice. Eve jumped. Whoever was speaking to her appeared to be able to read her thoughts! And the voice seemed to be coming from the tree! A little frightened now, she looked closer, then relaxed. A beautiful, golden-winged serpent stretched in the leafy branches, feeding on the tempting fruit. At least it was no fallen angel!

Without thinking much about how a serpent could possibly be talking, Eve answered its question. "We can eat all the fruit we want, except for the fruit from this tree. God said that if we eat it or touch it, we will die."

"Eve, don't you know why God told you that? Beautiful and intelligent as you are, He doesn't want you to enter an even higher level of existence. Instead, He wants to keep you forever imprisoned on a level where you cannot know all that He does. You are doomed, Eve, unless you eat some of this fruit. Why, just look what it has done for me!" The serpent paused to take another juicy bite. "Obviously, I'm not dead. In fact, since I ate this fruit, I've learned to talk! Just think what it might do for you!"

Gone from Eve's mind were the memories of God's wonderful gifts, of evening walks with Him, of shared sunsets and Sabbaths. Forgotten were the heavenly warnings against Satan, for it was the outlaw angel himself who was speaking to her, using the beautiful serpent as a disguise.

The pleasing voice continued, "Eve, you won't die if you eat this fruit! Instead, you'll be like God, Himself. You'll understand the difference between good and evil and know all kinds of things that you never knew before. Here, try some."

Eve's hand, so recently filled with flowers, reached out and took the forbidden fruit. She raised it to her perfect lips, formed by the hand of God. Her teeth, so white and pure, pierced the flesh of the fruit and the juice spurted.

The golden serpent flew away. As Eve stood, the fruit in her hand, she felt strangely excited. It must be happening! Just as the serpent said, she was becoming wiser. She would be not just the queen of Eden, but the goddess of the universe! Oh, Adam had to try this fruit!

Forgetting the flowers at her feet, Eve gathered all the fruit she could in her arms. She felt almost feverish. Her eyes sparkled and her cheeks burned.

"Adam! Adam!" she cried, as she rushed toward him. "Look! I've brought fruit from the tree. You know, that tree we've been avoiding? But Adam, I ate some and it's . . . "

His face went pale. With bloodless lips he whispered, "You did what?"

"Oh, Adam, don't look like that! I ate some, and I'm just

fine. In fact, I've never felt better! Adam, you must try some!"

He stared at his wife, not quite able to grasp what his senses were telling him. Eve had eaten the fruit. God had told them not to. If they ate the fruit, they would die. But Eve stood before him, laughing, radiant, alive. Her sparkling eyes held a secret knowledge, a knowledge that shut him out.

For one miserable moment, God's loving face flashed in his memory. He remembered the countless gifts that He had showered upon him and Eve. The words "Don't eat from the fruit of that tree . . ." echoed in his mind.

But Eve stood before him, still smiling with her secret knowledge, sweet drops of nectar still glistening on her lips. Never had she looked more appealing. Her eyes begged him to eat, and the tempting fruit, overflowing her slim arms, glowed in the sunshine.

Quickly he decided. He must know Eve's secret. What knowledge brought that sparkle to her eyes? Seizing the fruit, he crushed it in his mouth, and swallowed.

Suddenly the sky grew dark, the air chill, and the animals restless. The wind moaned, and Adam's and Eve's naked bodies shivered with a cold they had never felt before. Frightened and ashamed, the king and queen of Paradise skulked behind the bushes, trying to hide themselves.

In heaven the angels cried, and the tears of God streamed in the universe. But Satan laughed.

Trying to hide themselves from each other and from God, Adam and Eve pulled large, flat fig leaves from a tree, sewed them together with thin vines, and wrapped them around themselves. Their thoughts spun in a guilty whirl. They knew that soon God would, as usual, stroll through the garden, ready for His evening visit with them. For the first time they were not eager to see Him.

All too soon they heard Him calling them. Never before had He had to summon them. Why did Adam and Eve not run to meet Him? Why were they frightened and ashamed?

They had tasted sin, and its taste was bitter. The poison of sin had separated them from God.

"Adam, what have you done?" He asked. Adam, infected with sin, couldn't wait to blame his beloved Eve for what he had done!

"The woman You gave me tempted me, and I ate the forbidden fruit," he defended himself. (Not only was he blaming Eve, but he was also blaming God!)

"And you, Eve, what have you done?" God continued.

Eve, too, was ready to blame someone else for her sin. "Uh, the serpent that *You* made—it tempted me to eat the fruit!" she stammered.

Of course God already knew what Adam and Eve had done. He had seen their every action and read their every thought. But He had hoped that they would at least admit their sin.

Sorrowfully God told them what would happen because of sin. He began with the serpent.

"No more will you fly through the air on golden wings. Because you let Satan use you in his evil scheme, you will crawl on your belly in the dust. You and the woman will be enemies. You will strike at the heel of her offspring, but One of them will crush your head."

"And Eve, I created you as Adam's equal, but because man now has sin in his nature, he will use his greater strength to rule over you. You will have the blessing of children, but you will give birth to them in great pain.

"Adam, because you did not love Me enough to obey Me, the earth will no longer bloom and grow like this garden. Thorns, weeds, and thistles will seek to crowd out your crops and flowers. Growing food to eat will be difficult. You will sweat and grow weary until you finally die and turn back into the dust from which I made you."

"And," God continued, with tears still in His voice, "because sin now is in you, you can no longer live in paradise and eat from the tree of life. You must leave."

OUT ON A LIMB

Adam and Eve were tempted to eat the forbidden fruit, and because they decided to yield to that temptation, the history of the universe changed forever. While your decision about any temptation may not affect galaxies, it *will* affect your life in some way. Just remember—it's no sin to be tempted as long as you don't give in, and there's always a way out of any temptation.

Just as there was a way out of the temptation in the Garden of Eden, there's a way out of the tree maze below. Start at the fruit in the center of the tree and try to work your way out along the branches. You cannot cross any branch across your path, and you can't travel any one branch more than once.

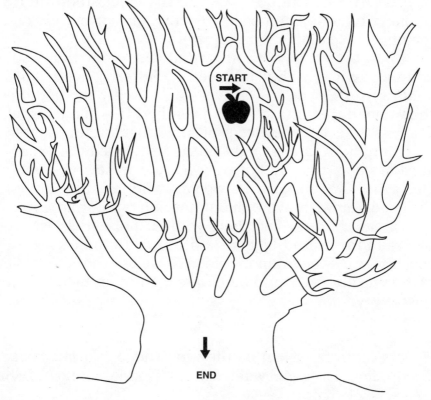

START

END

In amazement and sorrow the holy angels watched as the royal couple staggered from the garden. Weak with grief, Adam and Eve gazed for the last time on their paradise home. Each valley and hill, each riverbank and lakeshore was filled with memories of love and laughter and shining innocence. Each tree they passed, each flower, each beloved animal was the same. But they were not.

Yet God still loved them and cared about their needs. Now they must have clothes and the knowledge that their sins could be forgiven. Lovingly, he fashioned for them clothing from the skin of a cherished animal. With shocked eyes and drained faces, Adam and Eve watched the blood spurt from the dying animal.

Through tear-blinded eyes, the outcasts from Eden turned to look once more at the paradise that had once been theirs. At the gate a shining angel stood guard. Brilliant, blinding light beamed across the earth and sky as the angel held aloft a flaming sword.

It had been a day of sorrow and loss, a day that would change each one that followed it. Bitterly, Eve recalled Satan's words, "You will be like God!" If only she had used the wonderful mind God had given her! How gladly would she now trade her knowledge of sin for her lost innocence!

Painfully, Adam thought of the tree called the "knowledge of good and evil." If only he had trusted God more! His loving Creator knew he would be happy knowing only the good. Knowing evil brought nothing but unhappiness.

Yet God had not left them without hope. His love was bigger than sin and bigger than death. He had a plan to save them. As the animal's blood flowed so that the bodies of Adam and Eve could be covered, His own blood would flow to cover their sins.

❊ ❊ ❊ ❊

The room fell silent as the tape ended. No one spoke. Slowly, Stacey rose and walked to the door. Reaching out, she switched off the light, plunging the room into deep shadows.

Professor Appleby and the others heard her sigh. "It's like the darkness returned," she said. "Before God created the world, there was nothing. Then, after Adam and Eve sinned, there was nothing again—nothing but sadness."

"Oh, but there was hope," the professor called out. "Don't you remember the other stories Maggie B has told us? God didn't desert the world. For thousands of years He's been trying to save it. And someday He will, just as He promised.

"These stories Maggie B sends—the adventures and mysteries and miracles she uncovers in her travels—can help to remind us of how hard God is working against evil. My sister doesn't want her recordings to make us sad. She wants them to bring us hope. Don't you see?"

The room lights flashed on again. Stacey nodded, letting the old man's words sink deep into her mind. "You're right, Grandfather," she said. "Everybody needs hope."

Jason jumped to his feet. "That's it! That's it!"

"What's it?" Maria asked.

The boy began to pace back and forth, finger held high above his head. "Remember what we were talking about yesterday—about how Maggie B's stories are so cool that all the kids at school should be hearing them, but then we figured not everyone wanted to listen to stuff from the Bible 'cause some people think it's boring and only teaches about rules and regulations that are older than a redwood tree?"

"So?" Stacey shrugged.

"Don't you get it?" the boy pressed. "Maggie B's stories don't talk about rules and regulations. They talk about hope and stuff like that. She helps us understand that God hasn't forgotten us—that He still loves us even though we live in a world where weeds grow and people cry a lot."

"You're right," Maria said, her eyes growing bigger and bigger. "So they should hear the stories because of the hope in them—"

"And everyone needs hope," Stacey gasped, completing

Maria's sentence for her. "Grandfather! We've got to let other kids hear the stories. We've just gotta."

"Hold on there, guys," the professor called, waving his hands in the air. "Aren't you forgetting something?"

"What?" the children chorused.

"The townspeople. They think I'm crazy, and half of them are right." Stacey grinned at her grandfather's hidden joke. "So how are we going to get them to let their kids come out here to my old abode and listen to Maggie B's story tapes? They probably think I'd kidnap their sons and daughters and sell them into slavery like Joseph's brother did to him. Remember?"

The children's smiles faded. "Maybe you're right, Professor," Jason admitted. "But *we* know you're not crazy—a little strange, maybe, but definitely not crazy."

Maria looked into the old man's eyes. "But Maggie B would want other kids to hear her stories, wouldn't she?"

"Oh yes, she would," the professor nodded. He thought for a moment, then added, "It would make her very, very happy."

"Then we'll figure out a way," Stacey said, heading for the door. "But now we'd better get back into town before *our* folks think we've been kidnapped." She turned. "Don't worry, Grandfather. We'll think of something."

The children left amid waves and happy calls. As they hurried down the long driveway leading through the woods away from the old mansion, Professor Appleby stood on the front porch watching, his smile broad, his eyes sparkling.

"See you tomorrow," he called. "I've got more stories for you to hear."

After the children had gone, the old man walked back into the house and made his way to the den. Evening sunlight lay long over faded rugs and curtains, brushing tall shelves filled with objects from distant lands—treasures that his sister had sent during her far-flung journeys.

"I'm sorry I'm such a crazy man, Maggie B," the professor said aloud. "You want your stories to touch the lives of many children. I know that. But how? People aren't too sure about me. They don't know I'm just a lonely old man who lives in the forest."

His gaze fell on a portrait of a slender woman, eyes soft and loving, face tanned and wrinkled by years under the hot sun of far-off places. "I miss you, Maggie," he whispered. "I want to help you get your message of hope out to the world, but I don't know how."

The sun dipped silently behind the hill by the old mansion, casting the room once again into darkness.

Miss Baker

Hey, get down!" Stacey commanded as she grabbed her two companions and pulled them into the bushes by the path. The early-afternoon sun hung warm and friendly somewhere above the leafy canopy overhead. Birds sang their spring songs, trying to outdo each other with bursts of melody.

"What's goin' on?" Maria asked, eyeing her friend. "Have you gone nuts?"

"Yeah," Jason added. "Why'd you dump us in these bushes?"

Stacey said nothing and pointed in the direction of her grandfather's old mansion resting at the edge of the clearing. "Who's that?" she asked.

Her two friends saw a woman dressed in a dark brown business suit holding a leather satchel under one arm and standing rigidly at the front door of the house. Her almost-gray hair was tied up in a tight bun at the back of her neck, and a colorful scarf hung neatly from her shoulders.

"Maybe she's selling something—you know, like encyclopedias or magazine subscriptions," Maria suggested.

"Or maybe she's an FBI agent looking for runaway bank robbers," Jason enthused.

The girls turned and stared at him. "Well, maybe she is!" he protested. "She could be in disguise."

"Oh sure," Stacey giggled. "Like in real life she's a sumo wrestler."

"Look, she's knocking again," Maria interrupted, pointing toward the porch. "Let's get closer to see what she wants."

The three waddled like ducks around the perimeter of the clearing, seeking a closer and clearer view of the front door of Professor Appleby's mansion.

Just as they reached the side of the house, they heard someone calling from inside.

"Why are you guys knocking?" a male voice asked happily. "Just come on in. Door's not locked. Lost the key 'bout a month ago."

Stacey suppressed a chuckle as she and her friends peered between the porch slats at the somewhat heavyset woman by the front door.

The visitor knocked again, this time a little louder.

"Well, come on in!" the voice inside the house insisted. "What's wrong with you guys? You don't usually knock." Footsteps sounded from the foyer as the woman backed away a little bit.

The door swung open with a noisy scre-e-e-ch, revealing Professor Appleby's smiling face. "So what's with all this knock—" The old man blinked. "Hey, you're not the children. I thought you were the children. They come almost every day, you know. Been expecting them. Got the tapes ready. Stories. From my sister. You like stories? 'Course you do. Everyone likes stories. You sellin' something?"

The woman at the door stood with her mouth open, unable to interject a word, try as she might.

"I'll just bet you're selling perfume. I don't wear perfume. 'Course, you probably figured that out. But I've been known to splash on a little aftershave. Got any aftershave in your satchel?"

"Sir—"

"Oh, you can call me Professor Appleby. All my friends do. 'Cept I don't have a whole lot of friends 'cause folks think I'm a little touched in the head. Maybe I am, but it's not a bad touched. Just forgetful. Why, just last week I—"

"Professor Appleby?" the woman interrupted, lifting her hand as if to ask a question.

The old man stopped talking and smiled. "You must be a teacher," he said shyly. "Only a teacher would know how to get the attention of a fellow instructor."

The woman grinned and nodded. "You're right, Professor. I've been guiding minds for more than 40 years, and if there's one thing I've learned, it's this: a teacher will always stop talking if someone in the classroom wants to ask a question."

"And what might that be?" Professor Appleby queried.

"First of all, my name is Anna Baker. I know that wasn't a question, but I thought you just might be curious."

The professor held out his hand. "How do you do, Mrs. Baker."

"It's Miss, not Mrs. I've never been married."

"Really? A handsome woman like you never been married? Why, that's simply amazing."

The visitor blushed and cleared her throat. "Well, thank you. But I do have a question to ask."

"Of course."

Miss Baker looked past the man and peered into the brightly lit foyer. "Do you think we could talk inside? It's a lovely spring day and all, but—"

"Oh, where are my manners?" the professor gasped, stepping aside so his visitor could enter. "Please, do come in. You're most welcome in my home."

The two disappeared into the building and the children saw and heard the front door cre-e-a-k shut.

"Phooey! Now we can't hear them anymore," Jason complained in a whisper.

"I want to know what question that lady asks the professor," Maria said.

Stacey lifted her finger. "Hold on, guys. We're not defeated yet. Follow me!"

The children, still crouching like a flock of ducklings, waddled under the side window and hurried to the back of the house. Stacey led her companions to a small entrance cut into the basement wall. Pulling back a weathered wooden door, they slowly descended a small flight of steps and ended up in a dark, musty room with cement blocks for walls and hard-packed dirt for a floor.

"Oh, this is a nice spot," Jason whispered, eyeing the collection of dusty spiderwebs hanging like stalactites from the exposed beams overhead.

"Real cozy," Maria added, bending to miss a broken pipe jutting from the ceiling. "Come here often?"

"Quiet, you guys," Stacey said, lifting her finger to her lips. "They'll hear you."

"Whadda ya mean?" Jason called.

Stacey rolled her eyes and motioned for her companions to follow. "Just trust me," she breathed.

Maria and Jason shrugged and followed her through the shadows. Arriving at another flight of stairs, Stacey began climbing. Then she eased open a trap door in the ceiling and scampered into what looked like a small closet. Her two companions followed, groping their way in the darkness.

Once they were all up, Stacey closed the trap door, giving the three more standing room in the tiny enclosure. Maria was about to say something when they heard voices.

"And this is the den," the professor was saying. He sounded so close that Maria jumped. "As you can see, I store a lot of Maggie B's treasures in here. I keep the shades pulled somewhat and a humidifier running year-round. Some of this stuff is very, very old—and fragile."

"I should say so," Miss Baker agreed, her voice slightly distorted as it came through the closed door. "Just look at this Syrian tapestry. And this figurine—part human, part lion, part crocodile, part hippopotamus. Why, if I'm not mistaken, the original would be from Egypt. It's a representation of the goddess Taweret. Unbelievable! You have the makings of an astounding collection, Professor. Artifacts, or even high-quality reproductions such as these, should be in a museum—a proper museum. Don't you agree?"

"Yes," came the quick reply. "But neither my sister nor I are very wealthy. She spends all her money digging up this stuff, and I use what little retirement benefits I get just to keep food on the table and heat in the house."

"And that brings me to my question," Miss Baker announced with enthusiasm. Stacey, Maria, and Jason leaned forward in the darkness, holding their breath so they could hear every word.

In the room Professor Appleby motioned for his guest to be seated on the old, faded couch by the fireplace. The two settled themselves between a bust of King Tutankhamen and a lamp made from a twisted piece of driftwood found on the shores of the Mediterranean Sea.

"First, I have to apologize for a tiny bit of deception," the woman began.

"Oh?" Professor Appleby said.

"Yes. I haven't been totally honest with you. Truth is, I know exactly who you are. And I also know your sister, Maggie B. You see, she and I have been writing back and forth during the past few years."

"You and Maggie are friends?"

"Well, I've never met her, but I feel as though I know her. You see, I'm a history teacher at the community college—the one at the far end of town—and we're seriously contemplating putting together a small museum of antiquity. Nothing ornate, mind you. Just a place where our students and the community can go to catch a glimpse of the way the world used to be centuries ago."

"Wow," Stacey whispered, "a museum, right here in our town!"

"And the college staff has sent me out to find a place to begin work on our little project. We've followed Maggie B's travels, and believe that both of you could help us greatly. So will you help us set up a museum of antiquity?"

Stacey nodded vigorously in the dark closet. She knew what such an offer meant to her grandfather. For years he'd lived all alone in his aging mansion by the river. Now he was being given an opportunity to be a part of a wider community once again, just as he'd been during his teaching career.

"Say yes!" Stacey whispered, barely able to hide her excitement. "Say yes, Grandfather."

"I'll do it on one condition," she heard the old man say. "You see, I've got a granddaughter named Stacey. She and a couple of her friends come to visit me almost every day, and we listen to story tapes from Maggie B."

"Story tapes?" Miss Baker asked. "What kind of stories?"

"Oh, about Bible times and the people who lived then."

"Sounds interesting," the woman said.

"Well, the children have decided that more kids their age need to hear the stories. So, here's my condition. I'll help you with your museum if you'll let the tapes be a part of your community program. We'll invite as many children as want to, to come out to my home. You'll be the college representative. We'll play Maggie B's tapes, and while the children are listening, you and I can begin organizing the artifacts and trying to come up with some display ideas. What do you think?"

Stacey, Maria, and Jason held their breath. They could scarcely believe their ears. Professor Appleby was putting his whole future on the line for *their* dreams, not his.

"I don't know," Miss Baker said, shaking her head. "You say these stories are from the Bible?"

"Yes."

"But we're not a Christian college," she said. "We're only interested in ancient history, the movement of civilizations and development of cultures."

"The Bible is filled with information you could use," the professor urged. "Even if you don't believe Jesus was the Son of God, there are still important dates, names, and places mentioned in the Scriptures. It's an ancient document that tells us much about the past that we otherwise wouldn't know."

Miss Baker looked around the room thoughtfully. "Perhaps if I heard one of these stories," she said.

"No problem," Professor Appleby chuckled as he

jumped to his feet. "I've got a stack of them right here in my closet."

Before the children could move, the door flew open. The professor and his guest gasped when they saw the unexpected contents of the tiny room.

"There are three children in your closet, Professor," Miss Baker announced, clutching her heart and trying to restart her breathing.

"Hi, Grandfather," Stacey said, an embarrassed smile plastered across her face.

"What on earth are you children doing in my den closet?" Professor Appleby asked, attempting to catch his own breath.

There was a long pause. No one spoke. Then Stacey stepped forward. "We saw Miss Baker at the front door and wanted to know what she was doing here at the mansion, so we sort of snuck in through the basement, came up the trap door, and . . . and you've gotta help with the museum." The girl hurried over to the woman on the couch. "Please, Miss Baker. My grandfather is the best man in the whole world, and Maggie B's stories are really neat and teach kids about people who lived in Bible times and did important stuff for history."

"Yeah," Jason called, running out into the room and clutching the old man's tape recorder he'd found on the closet shelf. "Just listen. You'll see what she means."

Maria burst into the den, holding a box of cassettes. "We came out to listen to these this very afternoon. You'll like the stories. Honest."

A smile slowly spread across the visitor's face. "All right, all right," she said. "I can see you're enthusiastic about what Maggie B has to say. I'll be happy to hear a few stories."

"Yes!" Stacey shouted. "Hurry, Jason, plug in the machine. Here, Grandfather, you choose which ones." The girl paused, looking up into the kind eyes of the old man. "I'm sorry we frightened you and Miss Baker. But if you hadn't opened the door, I would have. You've gotta help with the museum. You've just gotta."

Professor Appleby slipped his arms around his grand-daughter and gave her a tight hug. "Miss Baker knows my condition," he smiled. "It's up to her—and Maggie B."

With that he sat down on a nearby chair and pushed a cassette into the recorder. "This is a story about two people who gave birth to a whole nation," he said. Then glancing at Miss Baker, he added. "It's part of history. And it's from the Bible."

✕ ✕ ✕ ✕

"Thanks be to God and praise the Lord!" 90-year-old Sarah sang as she worked about the tent. Standing on tip-toes, she stretched her arms far above her, then threw her head back and laughed.

Abraham, watching from the door of the tent, laughed, too.

"Oh, Abraham! Why didn't you tell me you were there?" Sarah exclaimed, both pleased and embarrassed that he had caught her acting like a young girl.

Abraham said not a word, but gathered her in his arms. As he held her, he knew he also held a promise—God's promise. And as he looked at her, he saw God's promise of a son first made to him 25 long years before.

Closing her eyes, Sarah smiled as she thought of the miracle she carried within her. She could almost forget the years of hope followed by disappointment while she re-mained childless. The scorn of other women, the feeling that somehow she did not deserve the blessing that God gave to them, the ache for a child of her own—all drifted away like a bad dream.

Sarah walked like a queen these days. Head held high, she moved among the servants, enjoying the new look of respect and admiration in their eyes.

One servant, however, did not think Sarah's pregnancy

was so wonderful. Hagar, dark eyes brooding, shared her thoughts with no one.

Although Sarah noticed Hagar's smoldering silence, her happiness was too great to let anything disturb it.

Ishmael, Hagar's long-legged 14-year-old, knew what was on his mother's mind, however. Although he had been favored and honored as Abraham's heir, now he would be forced to take second place. Ishmael too sulked and brooded.

One day as Sarah sang about the tent, her song stopped in mid-sentence and she caught her breath. A wonderful, welcome pain told her that God's promise was about to come true.

"Send for the midwife!" she called to a servant. The girl's slim legs flew over the ground, and she called to everyone she saw, "Sarah's going to have her baby! Sarah's going to have her baby!"

People came pouring from their tents and the fields. The word spread quickly from family to family in all Abraham's vast household. They still could hardly believe it. *Sarah, 90 years old, having a baby!*

Abraham's face turned into one big grin as he wiped his sweaty palms on his tunic. For 25 years he had waited for God to fulfill His promise of a son and heir. Now, today, that promise would become reality. He and Sarah would have a baby son!"

Sarah looked up, eyes shining, as the midwife entered her tent. "God has blessed me!" she smiled.

Buzzing with excitement, the women gathered around outside. Abraham walked a little way off. With sure, steady hands he selected stones as he had done so many times before. Carefully stacking them one on top of another, he built an altar. Later, when his son was born, he would bring a thank offering. Now, he knelt before the altar and talked to the Friend who had led him to the land of Canaan so long ago. "Lord," he said, "You are the only God. You deliver me from my enemies and forgive me when I sin. You keep your promises. Today You will give me a son, just as You promised! I will teach him to love and obey You, so that he can have the same happiness in knowing You that I have!"

Suddenly voices filled the air with excitement and a servant ran across the fields to him. Abraham met the man in a cloud of dust. "Your wife . . ." the servant panted, sweat streaming down his face, "your wife . . . !"

"Oh, never mind!" Abraham exclaimed as he gathered his tunic around his waist and sprinted like a boy to Sarah's tent.

"You may go in," murmured the midwife. With reverent steps and bowed head, Abraham entered. Kneeling by Sarah's mat, he reached out his hand to touch his new son. Sarah, face flushed and hair damp with sweat, laughed with joy. Suddenly Abraham laughed too, but his laugh boomed right through the walls of the goat-hair tent. Joy and laughter had come to live with them.

Abraham remembered a time when he had laughed at God's promise. And Sarah had laughed at the promise when the angels came to visit them. But now a baby boy, bathed with salt and oil and water and wrapped tightly in a new clean blanket, nestled in her arms. And Abraham laughed again, out of sheer happiness. "Little Isaac," he said softly, as he lifted the infant from Sarah's arms to his own. "Your name is Isaac, for that means laughter."

"That's a wonderful name, Abraham," Sarah smiled. "It will remind us never to laugh at God's promises, and also how God has given us reason to laugh with joy in our old age!"

No mother and father ever loved a baby more than Sarah and Abraham loved Isaac. Sarah hardly took her eyes off him, day or night.

"Why don't you let me hold him for a while, so you can take a nap?" a servant asked, but Sarah snuggled the child closer to her and shook her head. "For 90 years as I napped or worked I wondered what to do with my empty arms while other women held their babies. Now I have my own son to hold and love."

Little Isaac gurgled and smiled and grew. Everyone loved him, for he happily smiled his toothless grins at everyone. His cheeks dimpled and his dark eyes sparkled, and he laughed easily. Sarah said to Abraham one day, "He's such a happy baby. I wonder if he knows he's a miracle!"

"I don't think so," Abraham said, a smile lighting his own eyes, "but he certainly does live up to his name, for he spreads laughter all around him!"

But Hagar did not laugh with little Isaac. And Ishmael shot hateful glances at the baby that had taken his place.

The months flew by. Little Isaac began to walk. Soon he could say a few words. When he was about 3 years old, Sarah announced, "Isaac is ready to eat grown-up food. I won't need to nurse him any longer!"

"This calls for a celebration!" Abraham exclaimed. "We'll have a feast."

As Abraham had done for his three special visitors just a few short years before, he sent a servant to catch the fatted calf. Sarah and her servants slapped flat pancakes of bread dough onto the outside of the round clay oven. Other servants set aside goat's milk to make into yogurt. Then Sarah said, "We will have a special treat for Isaac. Let's cook dates until they turn into syrup."

The servants brought the sweet-smelling fruit, but Sarah would let no one else cook her special treat for Isaac. As she slowly stirred the fruit over the fire, her face reddened from the heat and her eyes watered from the smoke, but she kept stirring until the brown juice oozed from the fruit and bubbled in the pan. A wonderful aroma drifted into the air, and little Isaac came running.

"What's that?" he asked.

"That," his mother smiled, giving him a hug, "is something good—especially for you!"

Isaac jumped up and down and clapped his hands, then squatted by the fire to watch. But Sarah wasn't through. After letting the syrup, or "honey," as she called it, cool, she mixed it with some bread dough. Into the dough she stirred almonds and raisins, then formed the dough into little cakes, like pastries, and baked them.

"Are those for me?" Isaac asked, all smiles.

"Yes, for you!" Sarah answered.

All of Abraham's large household came to the feast. Everyone smiled as he or she watched little Isaac, the miracle child, wrap his chubby hands around the bread and meat and pop it into his mouth. When he drank grape juice from a goatskin bag, everyone clapped and cheered.

"No more baby! Now he's a big boy!" someone called, and everyone laughed. Little Isaac laughed, too. Abraham and Sarah laughed. But not a hint of laughter lurked in the eyes of Ishmael and Hagar.

✗ ✗ ✗ ✗

As the story ended, all eyes turned to Miss Baker. The woman sat in silence, looking across the room.

"Is there more?" she finally asked.

A smile tugged at Professor Appleby's lips as he reached for another cassette. "Yes," he said. "Lots."

"I'm listening," the woman announced and settled back on her couch pillow.

Stacey glanced over at her friends. What was the woman thinking? Had she liked the story? Why didn't she say anything more?

Maggie B's voice filled the room once again as her next adventure began.

✗ ✗ ✗ ✗

"Just look at the new heir," Ishmael sneered. "Doesn't he look like a 'miracle' with grape juice running down his chin?"

Ishmael paused to see what impression he was making. Several boys about his age had gathered around just to find out how far he would go in making fun of Isaac, but they didn't dare laugh at either of Abraham's sons.

"Shhh! Here comes Sarah!" one warned in a loud whisper.

Ishmael shrugged in an I-don't-care attitude, but he wandered off before Sarah reached him.

But Sarah had seen and heard, and not for the first time, either. Ishmael's mockery of Isaac had become a constant part of their lives.

"Come, Isaac," she called. "Come with me while I wash some clothes in the brook."

As Sarah scrubbed clothes in the shallow stream and Isaac splashed and played, she thought about Ishmael and Hagar. Ishmael's treatment of her son had become unbearable. Always a hot-tempered child, his jealousy of Isaac had made Ishmael rude and mean. And Hagar ignored his torment of Isaac.

She knew that she had been wrong to ask Abraham to have a child by Hagar. But Ishmael was Abraham's son, and God had promised him a special blessing, too. Silently, Sarah prayed, "What shall we do, Lord? Isaac is the promised heir, but Ishmael is Abraham's son, too. Ishmael and Hagar will not accept second place, and they make life miserable for little Isaac! What shall we do?"

Sarah lifted the dripping clothes from the water. "Here, Isaac, can you hold one end of this tight while I twist?" Isaac, with an eager smile, grabbed the wet cloth in his small, brown hands. As Sarah twisted the other end of the garment, he planted his feet farther apart and his little face grew red with the effort to hang onto the clothes.

"There, that's good enough!" Sarah exclaimed when no more water dripped from the clothes. "Ready to try another one?"

As she spread the clean clothes on sun-warmed rocks to dry, she reached a decision. As much as she disliked the

idea, she would talk to Abraham and ask him to send Hagar and Ishmael away.

That night, from long habit, Abraham and Sarah walked beneath the stars. Sarah's heart beat fast. She remembered as if it were yesterday how she had asked Abraham to take her slave to be the mother of the promised heir. The bitterness and pain of the years since that night seemed to press against her chest, and she could hardly breathe. Now it had come to this. How would Abraham react when she asked him to send away his first-born son?

"Abraham," she began, her voice a little shaky.

"Yes?"

"I have something to ask you, and I know you're not going to like it, but please, just listen until I'm finished."

Abraham nodded and looked at her curiously.

"I think we both know now that it was never God's plan

for you to have a child by my slave, but how were we to know? We both doubted at times that I could give birth to the child of promise!"

He nodded again, remembering.

"And we both know that Ishmael is not the child of promise. Isaac is," she continued.

"Yes," Abraham agreed, still wondering what Sarah had in mind.

"But Ishmael will not accept second place to Isaac. He teases him and mocks him and makes life miserable for all of us! And Hagar just laughs and lets him do it!"

Abraham frowned. He too had noticed Ishmael's mockery of Isaac.

"But what I'm asking you now is not just because I want to protect Isaac. You must believe that! I've learned a lot about trusting God since the time the angels visited our tent, and when I see Ishmael making fun of Isaac—our living, breathing miracle—I see him making fun of God's word, His promise!"

"What is your point?" Abraham demanded.

Sarah looked him straight in the eyes. "I want you to send Hagar and Ishmael away. Isaac is the child of promise, and Hagar does not recognize that!"

The blood drained from her husband's face as he stared at her in total astonishment.

"I can never part with Ishmael!" he exclaimed. "He is my firstborn son, and although not the promised heir, he is my flesh and blood! Don't ever think that I could send him away!"

Tears started in Sarah's eyes, but she did not say another word. In her tent that night, she prayed. "Dear God, I felt I was asking what would be best for Abraham's family when I talked to him tonight. Now I leave it in your hands."

Late that night as her husband lay on his mat, wide-eyed and restless, God spoke to him. "Abraham, I know you love your son, Ishmael, but I love him, too, and I will take care of him. I will make him the father of a great nation. Do what Sarah has asked, for Isaac is the son through whom I will bless all nations of the earth. Only by sending Hagar and Ishmael away, will your family find peace."

Tears coursed down Abraham's weathered cheeks as he remembered his happiness at Ishmael's birth. If he closed his eyes he could still see the boy's first toddling steps and hear his first baby words. Now must he send him away, perhaps never to see him again?

"Oh, God," he moaned, "this is the hardest thing You've ever asked me to do. Gladly would I again move to another country, or give up all my wealth, if only I could keep Ishmael!"

But God had spoken, and Abraham obeyed.

In the morning he summoned Hagar and Ishmael. Brokenly, Abraham explained that they must leave his household.

Fire flashed from Ishmael's eyes as he listened to his father's words. "It's all because of Isaac!" he stormed. "But I'm your firstborn! Your inheritance should belong to me!"

Abraham placed his arm around the boy's stiff shoulders. "Oh, Ishmael, it is not your fault that all this is happening. Yet, if you would try . . . if you would treat Isaac more kindly and accept him as my heir . . . the child of promise . . . !"

"But it isn't fair!"

Silently, Abraham loaded a big goatskin of water and some food onto Hagar's reluctant back. "God will care for you," he whispered, then with tear-blinded eyes, stumbled toward his tent. Once out of earshot, Hagar turned to Ishmael. "It's not fair, you know! It's not fair!" she cried.

Ishmael's blazing eyes met hers in shared defiance of God's plan.

But their anger cooled as their steps led them past the fields where Abraham grazed his flocks and into the desert. Hagar remembered another trip into the desert years before when her pride and Sarah's jealousy had driven her to a well where she had met the angel of the Lord. She was sure she could find a well again.

But the desert stretched on forever. The dry wind parched their skin. The hard clay soil burned right through the soles of their sandals and the stones made walking difficult. Their precious supply of water quickly dwindled even though they tried to drink but little.

Hagar and Ishmael staggered on. They talked little, for the effort was too great. But Hagar's desperate thoughts tumbled in confusion.

What will become of us? How can I find that well? Shall we go to Egypt, or throw ourselves on the mercy of nomads? Or will we die out here in the desert?

At last the sun dropped below the horizon and the heat of the day vanished with the sun. Now it was too cold, and the damp wind cut through their clothes. Huddled together for warmth, and fearful of prowling animals, Hagar and Ishmael spent a sleepless night under the cold desert stars.

In the morning they ate some bread and washed it down with a few drops of water. Then they put one determined foot ahead of the other as they faced the empty desert gradually warming from the morning sun.

Hot days and cold nights passed in a nightmare of thirst. "Where's the well?" Ishmael demanded late one afternoon, his voice hoarse and weak.

Hagar looked at him. He swayed as he spoke.

"It—it's somewhere near here! We'll come to it soon, I'm sure!" she promised with more assurance than she felt.

On and on toward Egypt they walked. One day Ishmael swayed and fell. Helping him to his feet, Hagar supported his weight with her own exhausted body. Half carrying him, she staggered on.

"Where's the well, oh, where's the well?" she moaned aloud, too desperate now to try to hide her fears from her half-conscious son.

Ishmael's head slumped on his chest. His dusty eyes seemed swollen shut, and he made no response to Hagar's groans.

Still the merciless sun beat down on the homeless wanderers.

At last Hagar spotted a few oleander bushes in the valley ahead, their fresh pink flowers strange in the waterless waste around them. With her last remaining strength she dragged her son to a bush and let him slide from her arms into the scant shade.

"He's going to die! He's going to die!" she cried softly to herself. Stumbling to another bush, she turned her back on Ishmael, for she could not bear to watch him die. But she could hear his moans, and she joined her own to his.

Then Hagar heard the voice of God. "What are you upset about, Hagar? Have you forgotten the promise I made to you? Ishmael will not die, for I will bless him and make him the father of many. He will, as I told you before, become the father of a mighty nation. Now open your eyes and look around you!"

Just then Hagar saw before her the telltale piles of stones marking a well.

Crying with relief and joy, she dragged herself to its edge. Tears of thankfulness ran down her cheeks as she filled the goatskin bag with water. Running to Ishmael, she wet his lips and tongue, bathed his face and eyes.

Slowly he drank. Ishmael would live. God had heard once more, just as He heard Hagar's cry so many years before.

In the years to come Abraham heard of Ishmael's achievements. His skill with the bow and arrow made him a hunter whose fame spread near and far. When it was time for him to get married, Hagar found a wife for him from her own Egyptian people. And Ishmael became a great nation, just as God had promised.

BIBLE PEOPLE

```
G Z T W L B Z F X X U F A R N B I N U Y
L K V S U X E P A V D H S M R A P E R X
F W P M O I S V O K K D J A B E H U A T
J V A Q A N B L E A H R Z R D U V I G P
C D W B O G Y R T J I A A X H M H R A H
A W B F L E O N K K E H R W D E E Z H N
T S U W E J V A K L A Z R G B B Y M J H
E Z H H U A M T E M W I W I E D I A A W
R K H M H G X A R L H Q A K W L C R X R
W I L S T D U S F A H V A J C O A N E T
D Q F A E Y P Q D I C H Q A B S Q D M A
P Y I C B B G T X L B H H A D K E L A P
U W S I H B E Y M L F Q E O C I G E F I
A I H L U C I F E R O Q U L W E R O X S
S N M I Q U O X W U V A E I B F J U V A
E Y A T Y Y H N P X R T V A P B R U W A
M J E V A Z Z W R H P O H H R A Y G A C
A D L C K C I Q K I K U H C A N N X U M
R J O A K F H G I N T X N A B A L Y F T
O Z D G H Q Z S L B Z F Q F N D A L X C
```

ABRAHAM   ESAU   ISHMAEL   LUCIFER   REBEKAH
ADAM   EVE   JACOB   MILCAH   SARAH
BETHUEL   HAGAR   LABAN   NAHOR   SATAN
ELEAZAR   ISAAC   LEAH   RACHEL

⚔ ⚔ ⚔ ⚔

Miss Baker nodded almost unperceptively as the tape ended. "It's true," she said quietly. "That's exactly what happened. Ishmael was the patriarch of the Arab nation, while the Jewish people can trace their roots back to Isaac."

"I've got one more story ready," Professor Appleby urged. "But if you have to go, we'll under—"

"As long as I'm here, you may as well play it," the woman replied. "While I'm not all that interested in the religious aspect of Maggie B's reports, they do contain much insight into the history of the ancient Near East. Please continue."

Stacey turned and winked at her companions. This was a good sign. Miss Baker wanted to hear the final story. The girl crossed her fingers as the adventure began.

⚔ ⚔ ⚔ ⚔

At Eliezer's soft command, the weary camels sank to their knees in the dust. The animals were tired after their weeks of travel all the way from Abraham's tents in Hebron to this city in northern Mesopotamia.

As for himself, Eliezer was tired, too, and thirsty. But his concern for the success of his mission gave him extra energy.

Then, floating on the evening air, came the murmur of high, clear voices. Eliezer settled himself under a palm tree while his gaze wandered over the landscape, strangely flat compared to the hills of home. But quickly his attention returned to the well-worn path in front of him, the path leading to the well. Soon young girls would file down that path for water, and he must observe them.

If the Lord willed, one of these girls swinging down the path, water jar on her head or shoulder, would travel back to Canaan with him to become the wife of Isaac.

Abraham had been very clear about what kind of wife he wanted Eliezer to find for Isaac.

"She must not be one of the Canaanite women,"

Abraham had told him. "I do not want Isaac to marry a woman who has no knowledge of the Creator God. Go back to Mesopotamia and see if there is a young woman from my brother's family who would be willing to marry my son. The angel of the Lord will go before you to give you success!"

Now the girls came into view. Some arrived in groups of two or three, others walked alone.

Eliezer prayed, "Lord, how will I know which young woman You have chosen to be Isaac's wife?"

Then he thought of something.

"This is what I will do!" he exclaimed. "I will ask one of them for a drink, and if she lets me drink from her jar, and then offers to bring water for my camels, also, I will know that she is the one You have chosen for my young master."

✗ ✗ ✗ ✗

Rebekah swung her water jar to her head. With long, easy strides she headed for the well. Other girls emerged from their doorways. Some had jars like Rebekah's; the rest had goatskins tied to the back of a donkey. In the cool of the evening they greeted each other and pattered down the familiar path to the spring. No one was in a hurry, for drawing water was a time for chatter, gossip, and laughter.

Rebekah breathed deeply of the cool evening air and hummed a tune as she approached the well. As usual, she stepped back to let some of the other girls go first. At last she descended the stone steps and brought the goatskin bucket, streaming with water, up from the well. Filling her jar and lifting it to her head, she mounted the stairs. But as she did, a stranger stepped forward to meet her.

Rebekah had never seen him before, but she knew from his tired and dusty looks that he had been traveling a long time. Nearby, 10 camels, burdened with all kinds of supplies, knelt in the dust, seemingly happy to rest.

"Excuse me," the man said, looking at her intently, "but

could I trouble you for a drink of water?"

"Of course you may have a drink," she answered as she poured water from her jar into his flask.

Eliezer drank deeply, but his mind raced ahead. The girl was kind. She was beautiful in a way that reminded him of Sarah, Isaac's mother, who had died a few years ago. Isaac still missed her.

But was she the right girl? Could she possibly be from the family of Nahor, Abraham's brother? Eliezer remembered his bargain with God. Would she offer to draw water for his camels?

As Eliezer lowered the flask from his lips, he felt his heart pounding. Would she turn now and walk away? He could not ask her to water his camels—she must offer to herself.

Rebekah lifted the jar, still nearly full of water, to her head. Eliezer's eyes questioned, but he said nothing.

Rebekah smiled. "Your camels must be thirsty. I will bring water for them, too!"

Eliezer's breath burst from him in a great explosion, and he realized he hadn't breathed since that last swallow of water.

With quick, light steps, Rebekah hurried to the wooden watering trough and emptied her jar into it. The water spilled along the bottom of the long trough, barely wetting it. She turned and ran down the stone steps again and brought the bucket up, sloshing with water. Splashing the water into her jar, she hurried with it to the trough.

As she poured once more, the water rose ever so slightly in the long trough. Again and again and again Rebekah brought more water. At last the trough was full.

Eliezer tapped the first kneeling camel, and it lunged to its feet and haughtily walked on its knobby-kneed legs to the watering trough. Others followed. A few slurps, and the water was gone! The animals looked expectantly at Eliezer from under their heavy lids.

But Rebekah was already on her way back to the well,

bringing more water. By the time all 10 camels had drunk their fill, night had fallen, her legs trembled from running up and down the steps, and her arms ached from pulling up the water bucket. But she smiled happily as she saw the camels contentedly chewing their cuds.

Eliezer had watched in wonder as Rebekah ran back and forth, without complaint, to water a stranger's camels. He felt sure this girl must be the one the Lord had chosen for Isaac, but he still didn't know anything about her except that she was kind, beautiful, and very strong! But he was grateful.

From the folds of his robe Eliezer drew some expensive jewelry, gifts from Abraham. "These are for you," Abraham's servant said as he handed Rebekah a gold ring for her nose and two heavy gold bracelets for her arms.

Her eyes grew wide. "Why—thank you!" she stammered, surprised almost beyond words.

"Tell me," Eliezer went on, "who is your father, and would there be room in his house for me and my companions to spend the night?" He held his breath again as he asked the question. Of all the girls in this whole city, could this one possibly be from Abraham's brother's family?

"My father is Bethuel, son of Nahor and Milcah," Rebekah answered immediately. Eliezer nearly shouted for joy! "There is plenty of room at our house for you and your men, and we have plenty of feed for your animals. You are most welcome."

It was too much for Eliezer—to think that God had led him straight to the granddaughter of Abraham's brother! Right there in the dust, with a few girls still lingering at the well, he knelt and thanked God.

"Praise the Lord!" he cried. "The God of Abraham has led me straight to my master's relatives."

Rebekah ran as fast as she could back up the path that led from her home to the well. She had so much to tell her family that she forgot all about Eliezer standing there.

"Guess what happened!" she exclaimed, all out of breath, as she entered her home. Her family listened open-mouthed, as she told of her experience. Laban, her brother, quickly caught the glint of Rebekah's gold ring and bracelets. Waiting to hear no more, he hurried to the well where Eliezer waited.

Just as politely as his great-uncle Abraham might have done, Laban greeted Eliezer and welcomed him. "Why should you stand here, you whom your God has blessed?" he asked. "Our house is prepared for you, as well as a place for your camels."

As Eliezer followed Laban to the home of Bethuel, Rebekah's father and all his family buzzed with excitement. This stranger who bore expensive gifts and who talked to the God of Abraham might very well be from the household of Abraham himself! And why had he given such valuable presents to Rebekah?

"Welcome, welcome!" everyone cried as Eliezer entered Rebekah's home. "Please sit down and have something to eat!"

Eliezer, however, had more important things on his mind than food. As Abraham's loyal servant he must first fulfill his mission. He thought of his master, so anxious to know that his son would have the right kind of wife. And he thought of Isaac, lonely since the death of his mother and eager to share his life with the girl whom the Lord would choose for him.

"I am a servant of Abraham . . ." Eliezer began, and the whole family of Nahor felt their hearts beat faster. Leaving out no detail, Eliezer told of his master's instructions to him to find a wife for Isaac from Nahor's family. He explained how God had led him to Rebekah, then asked her family if they were willing for her to go with him to be Isaac's wife.

Rebekah's father and brother answered quickly. "We can see that the Lord is leading! Of course we will allow Rebekah to go with you!"

Then Eliezer thanked God again, and gave gifts to Rebekah's whole family. They chattered happily as they examined the presents from Abraham. Jewels, fine clothes, bronze cooking pots, spices—all kinds of things spread around them like presents on a special holiday.

But then they looked at Rebekah and suddenly realized that they would be losing her. Her mother and Laban said, "Let Rebekah stay with us 10 days or so before she leaves!"

But Eliezer replied, "I am eager to return to my master, and would like to leave in the morning."

"Let's ask Rebekah!" both Laban and Rebekah's mother suggested.

Rebekah listened seriously as each person explained what they wanted her to do.

The girl's eyes misted as she thought of how much she would miss her mother and her family, but she knew that God had chosen her to be the wife of a man named Isaac, a man she had never seen, but one for whom God worked miracles. She felt honored and excited to be part of that miracle.

"I will go right away," she answered at last.

As Rebekah, her maidservants, and Eliezer with the other men from Abraham's household prepared to leave, Rebekah's family said a special blessing for her.

✕ ✕ ✕ ✕

Isaac walked back and forth in the rustling grass, avoiding the many thistles. An occasional raven winged its way across the blue sky. But Isaac's mind was not on the blue sky, the green grass, or the ravens. His thoughts were on Eliezer and his mission.

Many weeks had passed since the servant had left. Isaac wondered if a girl from his father's relatives had been willing to leave her family and travel hundreds of miles to Canaan to marry a man she had never seen. Most important, he wondered if this young woman would love the God that he loved and worship Him as his father had taught him to do.

Every day since Eliezer had left, Isaac had prayed that God would help the servant to choose wisely.

Then in the distance Isaac saw shapes like camels, dark against the shimmering heat waves. He shaded his eyes and squinted. As the camels approached he saw people—some riding, some walking. One person was . . . a woman! Excitement hammered in his chest, and he ran to meet the caravan.

Rebekah, from her seat high on the camel's back, spotted a man racing toward them. Good manners compelled her, in the presence of a strange man, to dismount quickly. As she slid from the camel, she veiled her face.

Isaac came closer. Yes, it was Eliezer! And he could see the woman who now stood modestly before him, her face veiled except for her large, dark eyes. His heart went out to this brave girl who had come to be his wife. After the formal introductions, he led her to his mother's tent, where maidservants waited to make her comfortable.

That evening he told her about Sarah, the lovely woman who had been his mother. He recounted the miracle of his own birth and how God had pledged that he, as Abraham's promised son, would have children who would be especially blessed by God. She, Rebekah, would be the mother of those children.

Rebekah listened intently, her eyes never leaving his face. She liked this quiet man with his great faith in the God of his father. And the Bible says that she became Isaac's wife and he loved her.

✗ ✗ ✗ ✗

Maggie B's voice faded into silence. All eyes turned to Miss Baker, who sat motionless on the couch. Outside, evening had crept through the forest and cast a soft glow on the spring leaves and branches beyond the big windows.

The woman walked across the room and stood before Professor Appleby and the children. A smile lit her face as she held out her hand. "I think we may be able to work something out," she said quietly. "Of course, I'll have to take this to the full college board for review. Why don't you stop by my office tomorrow around 10:30, and we'll discuss this in more detail, OK?"

Professor Appleby rose and shook the outstretched hand warmly. "Yes, Miss Baker, I'll be there. You can be sure of that."

The woman turned to leave, then paused. "Oh, and one more thing." She blushed slightly. "You can call me Anna."

"All right, Anna," the professor said softly. "I'll see you in the morning."

With that the visitor followed her host out onto the porch and then made her way to her car. With the turn of a key and a wave of her hand, she was gone.

The children stood in the doorway watching Miss Baker's vehicle disappear down the driveway. Stacey studied her grandfather for a long moment.

"You must be very pleased," she said quietly. "You won't have to be alone anymore."

The old man nodded, his eyes soft with the mist of happiness. "Maggie B's dream is beginning to come true, too," he added. "I must write and tell her." He smiled at the children. "Wanna help?"

The four turned and entered the mansion just as a mockingbird began its evening melody. The door sque-e-a-ked closed. Soon other sounds might echo down the corridors of the old mansion. Soon more children might come and sit together listening to the voice of Maggie B as she uncovered secrets from God's wonderful book, the Bible.

③

Seven Years, One Wife

"N o. Absolutely not!" Dr. Albert Morrison, the college president, tapped his finger on the conference table and frowned. "We're in the business of educating people, not converting them to Christianity. This isn't a mission station. We're a college. As it is, we've enough problems without jumping into a separation of church and state issue."

A week had passed since Miss Baker's visit to the old mansion in the woods. As promised, she'd presented Professor Appleby's condition to the full college board. The reaction of the institution's leadership wasn't exactly what she'd expected.

"Appleby and his sister aren't trying to convert anyone," she protested. "They're simply trying to bring Bible history to life—to make it more interesting to young people. After all, it's an important part of Western culture. Our literature teachers often find themselves referring to the Biblical narrative in their classes. Past writers didn't exactly ignore it, you know."

"The Bible does contain names, dates, and other information that have influenced us all," a former English teacher member of the board agreed. "I don't see how promoting a few stories could do any damage to the community. Margaret Brewster, or 'Maggie B,' as the good professor calls her, is a respected archaeologist. Her research is always professional and thorough. If she believes what she finds hidden in the soil of the Middle East helps to support Bible history and traditional Western values, shouldn't we listen and perhaps learn from what she has to say?"

"That's not the point," Dr. Morrison countered. "We're not a religious organization. If we start telling Bible stories

as part of our educational program—"

"They're not just Bible stories," Miss Baker interrupted. "They're *history* stories." She paused and smiled over at her boss. "Listen, Albert, I understand your concern. But if you could've been there last week, sitting in that old mansion surrounded by artifacts and treasures from the very countries mentioned in the Bible, you would've come away with a completely different idea of what the professor and his sister are trying to do.

"Yes, they are Christians. And yes, they believe God inspired the writers who wrote the Bible. Should that be reason to reject what they know, and the services they can offer to our college?" Miss Baker slowly looked about the room. "Since when are we in the habit of rejecting the generous help people offer simply because they believe we're supposed to love our enemies, live in peace, and forgive others when they make mistakes?"

Dr. Morrison leaned back in his big leather chair. "Aren't you being a little unreasonable here?" he said. "They can believe whatever they want."

"And so can we," Miss Baker added. "That's called good ol' American freedom. It's even in our country's constitution. Looked it up last night just to be sure."

Subdued chuckles echoed about the table as Dr. Morrison frowned even more. "I'm still not convinced," he said soberly. "Some in this community wouldn't look lightly at this institution using the Bible as a teaching tool."

"Then they haven't heard these." Miss Baker lifted a small package from her satchel and placed it on the table. With a flick of her wrist she sent the little bundle sliding the length of the long conference table until it came to rest before the stern-faced president. "Those are four Maggie B tapes. Story of Jacob, I believe. All that I ask is you listen to them. See if you can find anything that would disrupt the peace and quiet of our little town. Play them for your son Carl. What is he—10, 11?"

"Just turned 12," Dr. Morrison announced, a smile replacing the frown for the first time since the meeting began. "Got him some new software for his computer. He's a whiz on that machine."

Miss Baker nodded. "Then how 'bout you and Carl sitting down and putting Maggie B and her Bible stories to the test? I dare you."

The president's smile broadened. "You *dare* me? Miss Baker, no one has dared me to do anything since I was in seventh grade."

"Then it's about time," the woman said warmly. "Please, Albert. Listen to the tapes. For me. OK?"

Dr. Morrison glanced around the room, then down at the little bundle resting in front of him. "Sometimes I believe you're as crazy as Professor Appleby," he said. "But you're right. I shouldn't reject something I haven't even listened to, even if it is from the Bible."

"Thank you," Miss Baker said softly. "It'll mean a lot to an old man and his sister. And it just might mean a lot to this school, too."

The meeting adjourned. The college president slipped the package of tapes into his briefcase and walked from the room.

✗ ✗ ✗ ✗

That night as Dr. Morrison arrived home just before supper. he found his son Carl at his usual spot—sitting in front of the glowing screen of his computer.

"Hi, Dad," the boy called as his father entered the large library room of their home. "These new programs work great. Wanna see?"

"A little later," the man promised, sitting down heavily in his favorite chair by the window. "But first I want to ask you to do something for me."

The boy switched off his computer and turned to face his father. "You don't want me to do your taxes again, do you?"

"No," Dr. Morrison grinned. "That's not until April."

"Then what's up?" the boy asked.

The college president cleared his throat. "I want you to listen to something. Several cassette tapes."

"What's on 'em?"

"Well, they have some stories from the Bible."

"The Bible?" Carl blinked and stared at his father. "We've never listened to Bible stories before."

"Yeah, well, I guess we haven't. I'm not a religious man. I mean, we haven't had much need for stuff like this in our family over the years and . . . I mean, we do believe in God and all, but . . ."

"I know about the Bible," Carl said.

"You do?"

"Sure. There's this girl at school—her name's Stacey—and she tells stories she hears at her grandfather's house. Neat stuff."

"Oh, then maybe you'll like these." He held up the bundle of cassettes. "I asked Mom to bring us supper here in the library. Thought we'd eat and listen at the same time. Whadda ya think?"

"Cool. Let's do it."

"Yeah, cool," the man repeated, heading for the powerful sound system nestled in a cabinet by the door. He quickly inserted a tape and made some adjustments. Then hurrying to his chair, he sat down, propped up his feet, and waited for the story to begin.

✕ ✕ ✕ ✕

Rebekah absentmindedly twirled one silky strand of hair round and round her finger.

"Isaac, why do you suppose we have not yet had a child? God has promised us children, but we've been married now for 19 years—!" She wanted to say more, but she found no words to express her longing for a baby, or her confusion about God's promise.

Nineteen years! It seemed impossible that so much time had passed since she had left her family to become Isaac's wife. But, she thought quickly, she would do it all again for the quiet, gentle man who was her husband, and for the wonderful God he worshiped. But why did other women have babies so easily, one every year from the time they married, while she, to whom God had promised children, went year after year with empty arms?

Three deep creases, straight up and down, appeared between Isaac's brows. Those three lines appeared every time he thought hard about a problem.

At last he answered Rebekah's question.

"I remember my mother and father telling me of their long wait for a child. Years passed before God even promised my father that he would have a child, then 25 more years went by before that promise was fulfilled. I wasn't born until my mother was 90 years old! Everyone knew that my birth was not just nature at work, the way other children are born. They knew that God had performed a miracle.

"I hope we don't have to wait that long, Rebekah, but I do know that we can depend on God's word."

Isaac smiled into her eyes, and she felt better. Still . . . when would God give her all those children that He had promised to Isaac's father, Abraham?

Rebekah got busy. As she ground flour for the day's bread, her mind worked in rhythm with her hands. "God keeps His word, God keeps His word," she repeated to herself.

Suddenly Isaac stood at her elbow. "Rebekah, I need to talk to God. I may be gone awhile."

Isaac smiled, but she noticed those three deep lines between his eyebrows. *He's going to build an altar and ask God to give us a child,* she thought to herself. Aloud she said, "When you come back I'll have fresh bread and stew for you."

Later, as she peeled the hot, flat cakes of bread from the side of the hot oven, Rebekah looked up to see her husband striding toward her. The lines between his brows had disappeared.

God will answer our prayers, she smiled to herself.

In the weeks to come Rebekah realized that she finally carried a brand-new life. But as the days passed, she felt that something was wrong. The baby moved so much inside her that she felt as if it were fighting with someone! What could be wrong? Was her baby all right?

Troubled, she left her tent and the chatter of the servants and headed for the peace and quiet of the grainfields. As she sank to her knees on the sunbaked earth, the golden grain skimmed her cheeks and welcomed her into a private little world where she could talk out loud to God.

As she told Him her worries, His voice suddenly filled the silence and Rebekah listened in wonder as God spoke to her.

"Don't worry, Rebekah. Everything is all right. But within your body you carry not just one child, but two sons, different as sunshine and rain. One will be stronger than the other. Each will become the head of a nation, but the nations will be enemies. And, Rebekah, believe it or not, your older son will serve the younger."

Rebekah ran back to the tent to tell Isaac.

Weeks later a circle of flickering lights cast strange shadows on the walls of the tent as her servants held oil lamps around her mat. The time had come for not just one baby, but two little boys, to be born.

The midwife bending over her straightened and thrust a tiny form into Rebekah's waiting arms. The baby wailed and Rebekah smiled as she examined the little red body, all covered with dark fuzz. "Oh, look at my little hairy baby!" she exclaimed. "I'll name him Esau ["hairy"]!" But her words stopped short as another baby made its way into the circle of light in the dark tent.

"This one was holding on to his brother by the heel!" the midwife declared with a grin as she placed the second baby in the crook of Rebekah's other arm. "He grabbed that heel as though it was something that belonged to him!" she chuckled.

"Jacob . . ." Rebekah murmured. "I'll name you Jacob ["he takes by the heel," "he supplants"] for trying to grab something that wasn't yours!"

But the two baby boys didn't care what their names were, or that a circle of admirers examined them in the lamplight. They didn't know that God had special plans for them or how much their parents loved them. Nor did they know that great troubles lay ahead of them.

Jacob stuffed his fist into his mouth, and Esau yawned. Rebekah smiled contentedly. "Please go get Isaac!" she directed a servant. "He must see the sons that the Lord has given us!"

✕ ✕ ✕ ✕

Carl grinned over at his dad as the narration ended. "I'm glad that people don't name babies as they did long ago."

Dr. Morrison chuckled. "If we had waited to name you after you were born, you might be called something like 'He Who Cries All Night' or 'The Dirty Diaper King.'"

The boy laughed and ran over to the tape deck. "I like 'Carl' just fine." He slipped in the next cassette. "Maybe this will tell us more about those two brothers."

"What two brothers?" Mrs. Morrison called as she entered the room, carrying a large tray piled high with dishes of food.

"Jacob and Esau," her husband answered from his chair.

"Who?"

Carl eyed the contents of the tray. "The twins. It's in the Bible."

Mrs. Morrison glanced over at her husband. "The Bible?"

"Yeah," he responded. "Big black book? Lots of really thin pages?"

"I know what a Bible looks like," Mrs. Morrison chuckled. "Are we having a reading lesson?"

"Just listen, Mom," Carl said, pressing the play button and hurrying to his chair. As Mrs. Morrison placed her supper tray on a nearby table, a gentle female voice filled the room. The story continued.

✗ ✗ ✗ ✗

The sheep, usually slow-moving, broke into a run as they neared the well. Rachel made a sharp clicking noise with her tongue and raised her arms in a motion the animals recognized. Immediately they slowed down to a dignified walk.

Already, Rachel noticed, three other shepherds had arrived with their flocks. Purposely she avoided their eyes. The shepherd boys always stared at her and stumbled over themselves in an efforts to help her move the heavy stone that covered the well.

Of course someone had to help. The stone was so large and heavy that two strong shepherds working together strained and struggled as they half lifted, half rolled the well cover to one side.

Out of the corner of her eye Rachel noticed a newcomer to the well. A man, a bit older than the shepherds, stood talking with them. He led no flock. In fact, he seemed quite alone. A snatch of conversation drifted her way. "Why are you watering your sheep so early in the day, when plenty of grazing time still remains?"

Obviously the stranger knew something about sheep. But just as surely he knew nothing about the habit that the shepherds in this part of the country had of gathering all the flocks together so that they might help each other at the well.

Suddenly she felt the stranger's gaze upon her, warm and intense. Then he seemed to be talking about her, eyeing her and asking questions. Her sheep milled around, bleating, impatient for water. Abruptly he left the other shepherds, ran to the well, and with a mighty heave shoved the heavy stone aside. Rachel's eyes grew wide at his strength. But she turned her head aside as she again felt the man's eyes upon her.

Then, before she quite knew what was happening, the stranger was watering her flock. Quickly, with no wasted motions, he filled the nearby watering troughs. Expertly he controlled the greedy sheep, making sure that each drank enough but not too much. His hands, strong but gentle, held back the head of an overanxious sheep as it tried to bunt a smaller one. They lifted a lamb to the front of the flock, then lingered, just for a moment, on an old sheep, guiding it safely through the pushing, shoving flock.

Suddenly Rachel felt those same hands on her shoulders and a quick, warm kiss on her cheek. Shocked and confused, she stumbled backward, the blood mounting in her cheeks. It defied deeply held custom for a man to kiss a woman in public.

"Oh, please, the shepherds say you are the daughter of Laban. That means I am your relative!" he protested as she tried to back away. "I am Jacob, son of Rebekah, your father's sister. I have come all the way from Canaan. You cannot believe the problems I have met on my journey." His words ended in a sob, so thankful was he to have found his relatives at last.

Rachel looked into the stranger's face. His fine eyes, brimming with tears, held a question, an apology, hope, and . . . something more. For a long moment she gazed into Jacob's eyes, unable to look away. Then she smiled, that dazzling smile that scrambled the senses of the local shepherd boys and charmed all who met her.

"Please wait here! I will run and tell my father the news!"

Jacob sank to the ground. His long walk, more than 400 miles from his home in the rugged hills of the Negeb region of southern Canaan to the more rolling hills and flat marshlands in northern Mesopotamia, had left him footsore, weary, and lonely. But all through the long days and even longer nights he had felt God's presence. And now God had led him straight to the city of Haran, to the very well at which his uncle's daughter watered her sheep.

He had hardly believed his ears when the shepherds pointed out Rachel as Laban's daughter. As his eyes rested on the lovely shepherd girl, he had felt strangely drawn to her. His heart gave a great leap of joy. The news of her identity had filled him with happiness and excitement, so much so that he had tossed aside the heavy rock of the well cover as if it were a pebble. Now he smiled a little as he remembered his own bold, boyish actions. What must Rachel have thought, especially about that kiss? He realized, suddenly, that what Rachel thought was very important to him.

☒ ☒ ☒ ☒

Laban stared at Rachel.

"Rebekah's son? All the way from Canaan? And all alone, you say? Well, imagine that!"

Laban sprang from his seat on a soft sheepskin and

dashed out the door. Once outside the city, he hurried to the well. He paused as he picked out Jacob's lone figure, sitting on the top of the well. *Now, why would he come here all alone like this?* Laban mused. *Oh, well, time enough to find that out. My sister's son is here!*

Jacob jumped to his feet as he heard footsteps. Laban threw his arms around him and kissed him on both cheeks.

"Welcome, my boy, welcome. Come home with me and tell me all about yourself and your family. We must have a feast!"

Jacob gazed in wonder at the city of Haran. The great city gates, the long, low, houses of the rich, the beehive-like houses of the poor, the bustling bazaars with their strange sights and smells, all reminded him that home was far away. Yet this place held a kind of promise, and he felt welcome.

Seated comfortably in Laban's home, Jacob answered questions about his family. Yes, his mother was well, but age had worn heavily on his father when he had left . . .

Suddenly he found himself pouring out his whole story into his uncle's listening ear. He told of his longing for the birthright—that special honor and set of privileges that comes to only the firstborn of a family. Of wanting his father's blessing and support.

Jacob told of Esau's careless attitude toward the birthright. He confessed his guilt in deceiving his blind old father into thinking he was Esau so he could have the birthright and special blessing reserved for his older brother. And then he told of Esau's raging anger and promise to destroy him someday.

Laban leaned forward as Jacob told of deceiving his father. His eyes looked straight into those of his nephew. "And you say Rebekah put you up to this? But you did it, carried out the whole thing, right?"

Jacob squirmed. Behind Laban's polite mask lurked something that made him uneasy. But his uncle's voice held no reproof as he urged Jacob to continue.

Finally Jacob told how he had been forced to run away from his own brother, and of his fear that he might never see his parents again. Then he described his wonderful dream of the shining staircase with angels walking up and down it, and of God's promise to be with him always, even though he'd made a tragic mistake.

Laban listened carefully, his head forward, eyes half closed, but alert behind their heavy lids. His expression revealed nothing of his thoughts. When Jacob at last finished his story, Laban murmured, "You certainly are my relative."

Jacob gave his uncle a sharp look. Did Laban mean something he wasn't saying by those few words? But the man's face remained kind and courteous as he once more welcomed him to his home.

✕ ✕ ✕ ✕

"Doesn't sound like Jacob turned out very well," Mrs. Morrison said between bites of her fruit salad. "Sorta like the Carson boy—dishonest, running away all the time. Guess times haven't changed all that much since this story took place."

"Seems not," Dr. Morrison said thoughtfully. "Play the next one, Carl. I want to know what happened."

"You bet," the boy called happily, placing another tape in the machine. *This is neat,* he thought. The whole family was getting involved—a rare event in their busy lives.

As Carl hopped back into his chair and picked up his tomato and lettuce sandwich, a now-familiar voice began to speak.

✕ ✕ ✕ ✕

Jacob made himself useful at his uncle's house. Feeling at home with the flocks, he volunteered to help care for them. As he watched the sheep standing around in the afternoon sunshine, waiting their turn to drink at the well, he had an idea. Why couldn't the shepherds water their flocks in shifts, two flocks at a time? It took only two shepherds to remove the heavy well cover.

In just a few short weeks all the sheep grew fatter as they spent more time eating and less time waiting for their turn to drink. Rachel especially liked the new watering schedule that brought her and Jacob together.

"You don't have to help me roll the well cover away," he told her.

Without another word she placed her small brown hands on the rock and helped him lift and push the heavy cover.

"You *are* strong." Jacob smiled at her, admiring her determination. "But I still wish you'd let me do it alone."

"I like to help you," she replied simply, looking him straight in the eyes.

Gazing back into Rachel's eyes, Jacob felt he might lose his balance and fall into their dark, sparkling depths. Ever since that first day at the well, he had known, somehow, that this girl would change his life. As they had become better acquainted, the feeling had strengthened. Most men married for money or to advance themselves in some way. But from the first moment he had seen Rachel, Jacob knew he would marry for love.

He remembered his father's parting words: "Marry one of your uncle Laban's daughters." If only he could marry Rachel! But what did he have to offer Laban as a bride price? In Canaan he might be rich, but here he was as poor as any servant. But—he had an idea . . .

"Jacob," his uncle began that evening when they had finished eating, "you have been here a month now and worked as hard as any of my servants." Laban didn't bother to mention that since his nephew had arrived, his sheep were fatter, his servants happier, his household more productive, than they had ever been before.

"Now, why should I let you work for nothing just because you are a relative? Tell me, how much pay do you want?"

Jacob caught his breath. The very opportunity he had

been waiting for had jumped right into his lap! He tried to keep the eagerness from his voice as he answered, "I will work seven years for you if I may marry your daughter Rachel." Surely his uncle would not be able to refuse such an offer!

Laban glanced down at his lap, his heavy eyelids veiling his eyes like a curtain, a hand over his mouth to hide a sudden, secret smile. *Aha!* he thought to himself, *he's offered to work for Rachel, just as I thought he would. But seven years! That's a better bargain than I had hoped for!*

Aloud he said, "I can't think of anyone I'd rather have my daughter marry. It's settled, then. You will stay with us and work for me seven years—then Rachel will be your wife."

Rachel, listening behind the door, felt her heart begin to pound. "Leah! Leah!" she called as she raced into the cooking area.

Leah turned as her younger sister flew toward her. She felt a quick stab of jealousy as Rachel, with dazzling smile and flashing eyes, did a little dance all around the room. *Why couldn't I look just a little bit like that?* Leah thought regretfully.

Then Rachel stopped in the middle of a glide across the floor. "Oh, Leah," she breathed, "Father has promised me to Jacob, and I'm so happy!"

For just an instant a shadow darkened the older girl's pale eyes, but she managed to smile and say, "How nice for you! What kind of agreement did he and Father make?"

Rachel chattered on, telling her sister everything. Instead of giving their father a bride-price, Jacob would work seven years for her. And . . .

Leah's mind wandered. Seven years . . . would anyone want to marry her before seven years had passed? How embarrassing if she should still be single when her younger sister married!

For weeks she had watched Jacob, noting his helpful ways, and blushing whenever he happened to glance in her direction. Yet she had known, of course, that he preferred Rachel.

Under Jacob's care, Laban's flocks flourished. Soon Laban had to buy more slaves and hire more servants to care for all his herds. Wisely, he made his nephew his manager. Jacob cared for his uncle's flocks as if they were his own. At the first sign of a skulking wolf or approaching thief he grabbed his stout shepherd's staff and defended the sheep and goats.

At night, as he rubbed his hands together over a small fire, he often thought of his home and of his mother. He wondered if his father still lived, and if Esau was still angry. Painfully he remembered the day he deceived his blind old father.

Often he thought of the beautiful, shining stairway God had shown him in a dream, and he remembered God's forgiveness. But he couldn't forgive himself. Then he thought of Rachel, and the long, cold nights and the long, hot days passed like the blink of an eye. Months flew by like minutes, and the passing of years seemed only a few days to Jacob, for he loved her so.

On a sparkling spring morning when the last of the sheep had been sheared, Jacob approached his uncle. "Uncle," he began, his heart suddenly pounding, "I have completed my half of our bargain. I have worked seven years for Rachel. I would like to make plans for the wedding."

"Ah, yes . . ." Laban replied, his eyelids drooping sleepily. It seemed that he could not put Jacob off any longer. His nephew wanted to marry Rachel, then head back to Canaan. But he, Laban, would think of a way to keep the best shepherd and manager he'd ever had right here with him. "Well, of course, my boy," he purred. "Leave everything to me."

Laban's household busily prepared for the weeklong wedding feast. Sweets, fruits, and cheeses overflowed the cooking areas. Leah and her father had worked so hard on the plans for her wedding that Rachel had nothing at all to worry about.

"Only three more days!" Jacob whispered, a glad smile playing about his mouth. Unlike most couples marrying at that time, he and Rachel would marry for love—not convenience.

Then, just before the marriage feast would begin, Rachel listened in shock and disbelief as her father spoke. "You cannot marry before your sister does. Leah must marry first. Therefore, Leah, not you, will become Jacob's bride."

"Father! No! You can't do this!" she cried. "What will Jacob say?"

"Jacob will never know until it is too late. The night hides many things, and it will hide your sister from him. The heavy wedding veil will cover Leah's face, and like a proper, shy bride, she will remain silent."

"No, no, no!" she moaned. "You can't do this to Jacob. He has waited so long and worked so hard. How can you do this to him?"

"I have a feeling," Laban mused, "that Jacob may understand better than you think."

"Well, I don't understand, and I won't let you and Leah do this to us!"

"My daughter," his voice was chill, "you forget yourself. You will honor and obey me. If you have any foolish notions of telling Jacob about this, forget them. He might just leave for Canaan immediately, and then what would you have accomplished? Go along with this quietly, and at the end of their marriage week, I will arrange for you to marry him also."

The dawn's pale light found Rachel dry-eyed but trembling with exhaustion. All night long she had thought of Jacob—now married to Leah! "Jacob, oh, Jacob," she moaned softly to herself, "I don't think I'll ever forgive Father for this!"

Then a cry, dreadful in its anguish, pierced the still air, and Jacob staggered into the light. "What have you done to me? What have you done? Where is my Rachel? I've mar-

PIECING IT TOGETHER

Twice, Jacob worked seven years to make Rachel his wife. That's true love! Although Jacob encountered plenty of problems before starting the family he wanted and things may not have happened exactly the way God had first planned, Jacob eventually became the father of the twelve tribes of Israel, proving that God can piece together any shattered plan.

The puzzle below is really a maze. Beginning at the lower left corner, follow the black lines forming the puzzle pieces and encircle each of the seven spots throughout the puzzle. At no time may a line be travelled more than once. After encircling all seven spots you should end at the top right corner. Just as Jacob was patient in working seven years for Rachel, you may need patience to complete this puzzle successfully!

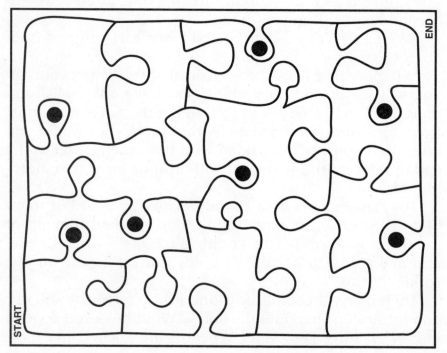

ried *Leah!* Laban! Where are you, Laban?" Then his voice fell to a broken whisper: "Rachel . . . Rachel!"

She groaned as she heard his words and felt his suffering. Then she heard her father's voice.

"There you are!" Jacob sobbed. "You tricked me!" But as he said the words, a look of pained understanding crossed his face. Was this what it felt like to be deceived? Had his father felt anything like this when he, Jacob, had deceived him? Had Esau known the same pain of betrayal? Had Jacob the trickster received his just reward?

He covered his face with his hands and listened to Laban's smooth words. "Yes, I tricked you, but it is not the custom here to give the younger daughter in marriage before the older. I'll tell you what . . ." Laban permitted himself a tight little smile. He had worked it all out so carefully! "You keep Leah as your wife, and at the end of the wedding week I'll also give you Rachel. But of course you'll have to work for her another seven years. Think of it this way: you will now have two wives who will give you a much larger family!"

When Jacob looked into his uncle's eyes, he saw his own reflection. *Trapped!* he thought. *Laban has trapped me!* Broken in spirit, deceived by his uncle, but still devoted to Rachel, Jacob replied, "I'll do it." But his words were bitter as he threw up his hands in despair. "What else can I do?"

✗ ✗ ✗ ✗

Carl wiped his mouth, then shook his head in disbelief. "Fourteen years? And all he ended up with was two *wives?*"

Dr. Morrison chuckled. "All I had to do to get your mother to marry me was promise her a new car."

"Now, Albert," his wife said, grinning, "as I remember, you also promised to love, honor, and cherish me."

"Oh yeah. That too."

The boy went over to the tape deck. "Don't get any ideas of shippin' me off to Uncle Pete so I can marry any of my cousins. They're a bunch of dodos."

"Don't worry," Dr. Morrison said, tossing a few kernels of popcorn into his mouth. "When it comes to your future wife, you're on your own. Just try to find someone who can support you."

His wife gasped. "You won't do any such thing, Carl Morrison. You'll find a caring, intelligent woman who'll be your equal in all things."

"Hey," Carl said, lifting both hands, "I'm only 12 years old. I hate girls, especially intelligent ones."

Dr. Morrison smiled. "Someday you'll change your mind about that, my boy. And if your're lucky, you'll find someone as smart as your mother."

The three burst out laughing and settled themselves for the next installment of the Jacob saga.

⚔ ⚔ ⚔ ⚔

For the hundredth time Jacob glanced fearfully over his shoulder. At any moment Laban and a troop of his armed servants might swarm over the hill and descend upon him and his runaway household.

Jacob smiled bitterly at the thought. He had arrived in Haran as a runaway from Esau. Now he was a runaway again—this time from Laban. Rachel, riding beside him, gave him a reassuring smile.

At least I have her with me, he thought. *But when I left Canaan I never dreamed that it would be 20 years before I'd be heading home again!*

Herds of cattle and flocks of sheep and goats plodded across the plain, away from Laban's grasslands. On the backs of camels, Jacob's other wives, including Leah, and their special servants slowly lurched toward Canaan. Other servants and Jacob's older sons herded the flocks while the younger children scampered about, sometimes running ahead of the animals, sometimes tagging along behind.

Jacob urged his caravan to travel faster. He had a head start on Laban, for his uncle had been away with his flocks when Jacob left. But by now Laban had probably discovered his nephew's disappearance, gathered his men together, and given chase. He'd be furious, of course. How many times had Jacob tried to leave, only to have Laban, through trickery, find some way to keep him there?

But God had not forgotten Jacob, and one starry night as he dreamed of his boyhood home and the parents he had left behind, God had spoken to him.

"I am the God who appeared to you at Bethel, where you poured olive oil upon a stone and made a vow to Me. Now get ready and go back to the land where you were born."

As Jacob listened to that wonderful voice, he knew that the long, weary, homesick years were at an end. The time had come to leave, for God had said so.

But now as the sun trailed its fiery fingers across the evening sky, Jacob knew they must stop and make camp for the night. Perhaps if they left very early in the morning, Laban might not catch up with them.

In the early-morning light Jacob moved quietly from tent to tent. "Let's go," he spoke softly, urgently. "Gather the flocks together. Don't build any fires to cook your food. We'll eat as we go. Hurry!"

But his words were suddenly swallowed up in a great clatter of loud voices mingled with the brays of donkeys and the clank of weapons. Then Laban, his squat figure dark and threatening in the dim morning light, leaped from his mount and stood before Jacob.

"Jacob, my son," he purred in the deceptive way that his nephew knew so well, "why have you deceived me? You know I would have liked to have given you a going-away feast if I had only known you were leaving! To think that you would carry my daughters off like captives of war—!" Laban paused to wipe a phony tear from his eye. "You didn't even let me kiss my grandchildren goodbye!" he finished dramatically.

Jacob regarded his uncle with a mixture of disgust and

admiration. What a performance!

But now Laban's voice took on a more threatening tone. "You know I could do you harm . . ." He looked pointedly at the men with him, standing at attention, hands on their swords. "But"— for an instant Laban's face shone with sincerity—"last night the God of your father spoke to me in a dream and warned me not to hurt you."

Jacob caught his breath. How wonderfully his God watched over him!

"I knew you left because you were anxious to get back home," Laban continued. "But tell me, Jacob, why did you steal my household gods?"

The question so stunned Jacob that he hardly knew what to say. Steal Laban's gods? He would never do that! But who had?

Not knowing how to answer, Jacob stalled. "I didn't tell you I was leaving because I was afraid you would take your daughters away from me," he mumbled. Then, with a return of confidence, he exclaimed, "But if you find anyone in my camp who has your gods, that person will be put to death!"

Rachel, listening from her tent, felt the color drain from her face. Her eyes darted to a pile of blankets where she had hidden her father's household gods. Leah had been blessed with many children, but Rachel was afraid that she would never have any. *Maybe,* she had thought at the time she had taken them, *my father's fertility gods will help me to bear children.*

Now Laban roared to his servants, "Search the tents. Leave nothing unturned. We will find those gods before we leave here!"

Rachel peeked out of her tent. Ah! The search had begun in a tent far from hers. She had time, just a little time—!

Her father and his servants stormed through the camp. The men tore into neatly stacked blankets, bags of cooking pots, baskets of grain. They tossed clothing around and knocked the stakes out from under the tents. Jacob followed, his face grim.

Finally Laban came to Rachel's tent. She sat quietly on a camel's saddle, hiding the household gods. She did not rise as her father entered, but he was so intent on his search that he hardly glanced at her. Again he overturned baskets, rummaged through blankets and clothes, peeked into every little corner and cranny of the tent. At last he straightened and glared at her.

Rachel smiled. "Forgive me, Father, for not standing. I'm not feeling well this morning."

Baffled, Laban stormed from the tent. He had searched everywhere! Slowly Rachel let out a shaky breath and shifted her position. She would have to sit on the little household gods a while longer until she was sure Laban had gone.

Suddenly all Jacob's pent-up anger exploded.

"You've hunted me down like a common criminal!" he

told his uncle. "You've ransacked my camp and invaded our privacy! You've accused me of stealing, and what have you found? Bring out all the stolen goods! Go ahead! Set them all right here in the middle of the camp so everyone can see! Oh! You mean you didn't find anything that belonged to you?" Jacob gave a short little laugh.

"I can't believe you, Laban. I've worked for you faithfully for 20 years. I never ate any rams from your flock, as most shepherds have the right to do. I took care of your flocks so well that the goats and sheep have multiplied every year. I risked my life many a time to save your animals, and if I did lose one, you insisted that I pay for it—not you." His face was white with anger, but his dark eyes blazed as he remembered the misery of the past 20 years.

"For 20 years, *20 years,* Laban, I suffered from the heat of the day and the cold of the night. I couldn't sleep at night, for I was always watching for danger. Fourteen years I worked for your daughters. Six more years I worked for your flocks. But even then you kept changing my rate of pay—and always to your advantage!"

Laban's half-closed eyes revealed nothing. He raised a hand as if to quiet Jacob, but his nephew had more to say.

"If it had not been for the mercy of my God, the God of Abraham and Isaac, you would have sent me away empty-handed. But God has seen my trouble and the work I've done, and that is why He gave you a dream last night—a dream to keep you from destroying your own relatives!"

Laban studied his nephew's angry face from behind veiled eyes. Suppose Jacob joined up with his brother Esau, a mighty warrior, and returned to attack him? *I'd better see what I can do to smooth this over,* he thought. *But I won't admit doing anything wrong!*

"Jacob," he began, his tone friendly and peaceful, "your wives and their children belong to me. Your flocks are mine. In fact, everything here belongs to me." His nephew felt the hot blood rush to his temples, but Laban hurried on.

"But I'm ready to make an agreement with you. Why don't we set up a memorial, a pile of rocks that will be a reminder to both of us that we won't go beyond this point to attack each other?"

Laban's peaceful words did not fool Jacob. *He's afraid I'll come back and raid him, because that is what he would do to me!* Jacob thought. But he agreed.

Both men quickly gathered a pile of rocks. As they worked together, picking up the stones and wedging them on top of each other, Jacob looked at his father-in-law. Could there still be friendship between them? Would his uncle at last confess his wrongs to Jacob and ask forgiveness? But Laban's eyes, beneath their sleepy lids, were as cold and hard as the stones he handled.

At last Laban spoke. "This pile of rocks and this memorial stone will forever be a reminder of the promises we make to each other this day. I promise that I will not go beyond this point to attack you. You must promise the same to me. And may your God watch you to make sure you keep your promise."

Jacob permitted himself a little smile, but he solemnly promised. Then he offered a sacrifice to God and prepared a big meal for Laban's men as part of the covenant. The next morning Laban strolled through the camp, stopping to kiss his grandchildren goodbye and say farewell to his daughters.

Once more fixing his sleepy gaze on Jacob, he drawled, "May the Lord keep an eye on us while we are separated."

Then, with a quick leap to the back of a donkey, he rode away, his squat form getting smaller and smaller in the distance, finally disappearing in a cloud of dust.

✗ ✗ ✗ ✗

When the story ended, Dr. Morrison turned to his son. "What do you think of those tapes?" he asked.

Carl nodded enthusiastically. "They're great. Have any more?"

"No. Just those, though I'm sure that there must be more stories about Jacob and his family." He paused for a moment. "If you could hear more stories, would you want to?"

"Sure. They're kinda different."

"What do you think, Ellen?" the man said, addressing his wife. "Are these the type of stories you want Carl to hear?"

The woman leaned back in her chair. "I guess what I like most about them is that they don't glorify violence and hate like so much of the junk seen on television or brought home from the video stores nowadays." She tilted her head to one side. "Why are you asking us these questions? Are there more of these tapes? Who has them? Where'd they come from?"

The man lifted his hand. "All in good time," he said. Turning to the boy, he added, "Hey, Carl. Wanna go with your dad on a visit tomorrow afternoon?"

"Who we gonna see?"

"Oh, just a man. A crazy old man."

Ancient Mealtime

The story of Esau selling his birthright for a pot of lentil stew is unusual in that women normally did the cooking in Bible times, but the meal was typical. People of Bible times generally ate vegetables and grain—rarely meat. Meat was most commonly used as a flavoring for something else rather than as the main course itself.

Sheep and cattle were too valuable to eat regularly. The flocks were a family's wealth, and they could not afford to waste them as food. People saved meat for special occasions—weddings, religious feasts, or special celebrations (such as the prodigal son's return). In Old Testament times eggs came from ostriches or wild game birds. The chicken was apparently first introduced to Palestine by the Persians. Even after people started raising chickens in Palestine, they considered eggs as food only for children.

Those living near the Mediterranean coast or the Sea of Galilee could catch fish, but the only way they had of preserving it was to salt and dry it.

Because cooking was slow and difficult, the women prepared the meals while the men were working in the fields. They heated food over wood fires and baked the flat loaves of bread with small clay ovens. Because there were no ways of preserving food other than with salt or by drying, food had to be prepared fresh every day.

Each day the women would grind flour from wheat, barley, millet, or spelt on stone saddle querns, or grinding stones. Grain could also be roasted and then either crushed or eaten whole. The women would milk goats and sheep for milk to drink or to make into curds, a form of yogurt called leben.

Breakfast and lunch usually consisted of bread, fruit, and cheese. The main meal took place in the evening, when people could sit around leisurely and talk.

Besides lentils, which the people ate as pastes, purees, and baked in cakes, they had beans, leeks, onions, horsebeans, garden peas, and cucumbers. Archaeologists often uncover garbanzos (chickpeas). Garlic and other spices and herbs such as dill, mint, cumin, rue, anise, coriander, fenugreek, mustard, purslane, bay leaves, and cinnamon flavored the limited number of main ingredients. Although the Bible does not mention it, archaeological evidence indicates that thyme was especially popular.

Nuts such as almonds, walnuts, and pistachios were a source of protein and cooks often put them into their stews. Also they ate stone-pine seeds and roasted the seeds of the terebinth trees. Ripe olives served as a food, and the oil squeezed from them was used in cooking and for burning in the tiny clay lamps. Linseed was another source of cooking oil. People would eat carob pods, especially during times of famine.

Bread was the main food at every meal. It might be wrapped around the other food, or the flat loaves might be split open and the food put inside to make a pita sandwich. Because bread was such an important part of every meal, the phrase "eating bread" meant the same thing as having a meal.

Sugar was not known in the biblical world. To satisfy their sweet tooth, people had fruits such as quinces, apricots, dates, grapes, and pomegranates. The seeds of the pomegranate could also be squeezed to make a drink. Pressed cakes of figs made an easy-to-carry snack food. The poor would eat sycamore figs. Grapes were dried and pressed into cakes too.

Although people in the Holy Land apparently did not raise bees as the Egyptians did, they would collect the honey they found in wild hives. Also they apparently boiled a syrup from grapes or figs to the consistency of molasses that they could then use as a sweetener.

The people of the Bible did not use spoons and forks as

we do now, but would eat with their hands or scoop food up with bread. Families and guests would eat together from a common pot or dish. Nor did they sit on chairs at tables. Instead they would sit on the ground or lounge on rugs or mats.

④
Wheat Field

Stacey, Maria, and Jason sat staring at the strange object in front of them. Never before had they seen such a device, much less been able to lay their hands right on it.

"Careful," Professor Appleby warned, "that part is sharp. Has to cut cleanly and evenly, you know."

"But," Jason queried, scratching his short, black hair, "how did it attach to the tractor? You said it was a farming tool."

The professor laughed. "They didn't have tractors in Ruth's day. Only these."

"But what exactly is it?" Maria asked, eyeing the gently slanted piece of wood with what looked like stones embedded along the inside curve.

"Maggie B said she found the original of this on a dig near the town of Bethlehem. That's right, Bethlehem, where, many years after someone discarded this tool, Jesus was born. Said she found several, so the government ruling that area allowed her to keep one for her own private collection. The wood was so fragile, however, that she had someone make this copy of it. Neat, huh?"

"But what is it?" the three children chorused.

"Yes," another voice added from nearby, "what is it, Professor Appleby?"

The professor and children spun around to see a man and young boy walking in their direction. "We didn't find anyone home at the house and were about to leave when we heard voices out here in the pasture. Didn't mean to startle you all."

"And who might you be?" Professor Appleby asked, walking forward, the strange tool in hand. The strangers stopped, eyes fixed on the lethal-looking object held carefully in the old man's grasp.

"I'm Dr. Morrison, president of the community college. And this is my son, Carl."

"Hey, I know you," Stacey said, walking up to the younger of the two visitors. "Don't you go to my school?"

"Yes," Carl answered with an uncertain smile. He pointed at the device in the professor's hand. "Is he going to hurt us with that?"

"No, silly. It's something his sister, Maggie B, sent from the Middle East. She's always digging up old stuff. My grandfather was about to tell us what it is and show us how it works."

"Whew," Carl breathed. "Looks kinda dangerous."

"I guess it does," the old man agreed with a smile. Turning to the boy's father, he said, "Say, Dr. Anderson—"

"Morrison."

"What's that?"

"My name is Morrison."

"It is? Well. I was just talking to a Dr. Morrison this morning. Said he was going to come out for a visit. Have you seen him?"

The younger man blinked. "That was me. I mean, I'm me."

"Well of course you are. If you weren't you, you'd be someone else."

The visitor looked as if he was about to say something, then shook his head. "I'm Dr. Morrison from the community college," he said slowly. "I called you this morning to make an appointment with you. So here I am."

"Right on time, too," Professor Appleby nodded cheerily.

Dr. Morrison glanced at Stacey and the others. "Are you following this?"

Stacey giggled. "Of course." Then she ran to her grandfather, a little concerned in the presence of the man who could make or break the idea of a museum in the town.

"You were showing us that thing in your hand,

Grandfather," she whispered. "Maggie B found the original of it in Bethlehem? Has something to do with Ruth?"

"Oh, this!" the Professor laughed. "Of course. As I was saying, it's made out of wood and, look here, see those sharp stones embedded on this one side? Well, that's flint. They form the blade used for cutting grain at harvest." The old man walked a few paces into some tall grass. "All you do is swing it like this, and watch what happens."

With a wave of his arm, the professor swept the device through the standing blades. The top two feet of the grass separated cleanly and fell with a soft swish to the ground. "See? It's a sickle. A very, very old type of sickle."

"Oh," Maria nodded. "I get it. Farmers used it to bring in their crops. It must have taken them a long time."

"Not if you had lots of workers, and each one swung one of these. They could level an acre field in no time, just like in the story of Ruth."

Professor Appleby motioned for everyone to join him in the shade of a tall oak. "Jason, you set up the recorder. I put some fresh batteries in it last night. And Stacey, you stick in the tapes. We'll hear what Maggie B has to say about a woman named Ruth." Turning to the two visitors, he added, "And you guys can join us. But keep your eye on the driveway. I'm expecting guests."

Dr. Morrison sighed and shrugged. There was something about the old man he liked, something comforting, even in the confusion he created. The college administrator's son had already taken his place by Stacey and the others. Morrison figured any conversation he wanted to have with the old professor could wait.

The warm afternoon breezes warmed the grasses and sent flickering shafts of light through the leaves overhead as Maggie B's energetic voice cut through the fresh spring air.

✗ ✗ ✗ ✗

Naomi and Elimelech stared into each other's worried

eyes. The rains had failed, and where tender green shoots of barley should have been poking up through the ground, the dusty soil lifted into the air with every gust of wind.

As she thought of her two boys, Mahlon and Chilion, Naomi swallowed hard. "We can get by on less food, Elimelech, but the boys can't," she sighed, as images of their thin bodies flashed through her mind.

Elimelech's dark eyes reflected her thoughts. God had been good to them, but for some reason both boys had been sickly since birth. They would starve more quickly than other children. "There's only one thing to do," he finally answered. "We must go elsewhere."

Naomi caught her breath. She had lived in Bethlehem of Judah all her life. Her family and friends lived in Bethlehem. But she thought of her two sons, and the chance that they might go hungry gave her the courage she needed. "Where will we go?" she asked quietly.

His brow furrowed. "I've been thinking about that. The country of Moab isn't that far away, just on the other side of the Jordan. And . . ."

"Moab!" Naomi interrupted. "You want to take our boys to that land of wicked women and idol worship?" She stared at him with wide, astonished eyes. "Why Moab?" she demanded.

Elimelech almost smiled. His wife's quick wits and tongue delighted him, even now. But he answered her question with just one of his own: "How often have you heard of famine striking the land of Moab?"

Her eyes reluctantly gave him her answer. Glancing in the direction of her sons, she declared, "We will go to Moab."

Naomi soon settled into her new life in a new country. Happily, she found that the Moabites spoke a language almost like her own. True enough, many worshiped idols and took part in evil ceremonies. But she and Elimelech stayed true to God and soon won the friendship and respect of their neighbors.

Best of all, Mahlon and Chilion had plenty to eat. And they grew quickly. In fact, they were fast becoming young men.

But in the midst of her happiness, sadness struck again. One morning Elimelech lay very still on his mat. Naomi tiptoed about, not wanting to wake him. But as the sun climbed higher, she began to worry. Her husband never slept this late.

Gently she shook his shoulder. But he didn't move, didn't moan, didn't breathe. A cry escaped her throat, and she rocked back and forth in grief. Elimelech was dead.

Mahlon and Chilion worked hard to support their mother just as their father had done. Before long each son asked her permission to marry a Moabite girl. Naomi worried and prayed. Would the Moabite women lead her sons into idol worship?

But she welcomed them into her home. Orpah, with her soft voice and quiet ways, soon won her heart. Ruth, on the other hand, made her laugh as she hadn't since Elimelech had died. The girl's brown eyes twinkled as she told Naomi stories from her childhood, or mimicked the high-pitched whine of a street merchant. And all the time she flew about the home, straightening, cooking, weaving, her busy hands always finding something to do.

In the quiet of the evening, as the family gathered about the fire, Naomi told her daughters-in-law stories about Judah and Bethlehem and the God of Israel. Orpah listened quietly, thoughtfully, while Ruth's eager eyes, dancing in the firelight, never left her mother-in-law's face. She was thrilled to belong to this new family with its interesting God.

And Naomi went to bed happy. Now she had not only two sons, but two daughters-in-law who loved her and who had begun to love her God.

Then sickness swept the village. Suddenly it was in their own home. Mahlon and Chilion, never strong, burned with fever. And all the efforts of the three women could not save them. Naomi watched helplessly as her two sons grew sicker and sicker, until, at last, they died.

Pale, suddenly old, Naomi faced her daughters-in-law. "Our situation is desperate," she stated bluntly. "I have no husband and no sons to support me. Nor do I have any male relatives here to turn to.

"Your situation is not much better than mine, but you are young. There's a chance that you might marry again. So let us part. I will go back to Bethlehem, for the famine has long since passed. My family and friends there might take pity on me. And you, my daughters, must stay here and return to your homes."

Orpah and Ruth began to cry. Naomi, now bowed with sorrow, had become like a mother to them. How could they watch her walk away, alone, into the wilderness that lay between Moab and Bethlehem?

"We will come with you!" they exclaimed. Naomi had not the strength to object, and the three women, a sad and quiet little group, set out on the road toward Judah with a small caravan of merchants for protection.

At last they reached the border of Moab, and Naomi gathered the strength to insist once more, "My daughters, you must turn back. I can promise you nothing in Judah. I have no other sons for you to marry through the law of levirate marriage, nothing at all to give you. You must return to your own homes."

Orpah struggled with her feelings. But at last she threw her arms around her kind and wise mother-in-law and kissed her goodbye. Then, sorrowfully, she turned back toward Moab. Some passing merchants were heading back east, and she would return with them.

But Ruth stood as unmovable as a rock. In a voice that shook with love and determination, she cried, "Please don't ask me to leave you. Where you go, I will go. Where you stay, I will stay. Your people will be my people, and your God my God. And may the Lord deal most cruelly with me if I allow anything but death to separate us!"

Naomi's face crumpled as all the grief she had long held back sent tears coursing down her cheeks. And to think that she had once thought all Moabite women were wicked! At last she smiled through her tears, and supported by Ruth's strong young arm, once more turned her steps toward Judah.

For days they walked over the rugged mountains, carrying their few belongings on their heads, and warmed by the bright spring sunshine. At night they shivered under their cloaks, then rose to face another day of their difficult journey. At last they reached the Jordan, and finding a place to ford, they lifted their skirts and waded across with the rest of the merchant caravan.

TRACE OF LOYALTY

Ruth's willingness to follow Naomi from Moab to Israel is an example of true loyalty. Can you follow Ruth's famous declaration of loyalty through the jumble of letters below? Trace this quote from Ruth by starting at the arrow then moving one square at a time in any direction to join the letters in the correct order. You may move to the right, left, up, down, or diagonally, but do not cross any letter more than once. All the letters must be used and you should end in the bottom right corner of the puzzle.

START →T	P	E	M	Y	Y	G
H	Y	E	B	P	E	H	O
L	O	L	P	O	T	D	M
P	E	L	L	E	D	G	Y
S	H	A	A	N	O	D → END

Then they began to climb until at last Naomi spotted the hills of Bethlehem, vivid with springtime green. Her mind spun with a thousand thoughts as she and Ruth approached the gate of the dusty little town. How full her life had been when she'd left with her husband and two boys. Now she felt that she had returned with nothing, despite the lovely Moabite girl at her side.

She glanced at Ruth. Did she realize, she wondered, what lay in store for her? In Judah no one trusted a Moabite woman. They were looked down upon even more than most foreigners. Naomi felt a catch in her throat. If only they could know Ruth as she did!

The gate swung open, and they walked inside. The townspeople stared at the two travel-weary women. Then they gathered around, all talking at once.

"Naomi! Is that you? But you've changed so! Where is your family? And who is that? What has happened, Naomi? Tell us everything!"

A bitter smile touched Naomi's lips, not quite reaching her eyes. "Yes, I've changed. You knew me as Naomi, the 'pleasant one.' But don't call me that now. Call me Mara, the 'bitter one,' for I went away full and came back empty."

✗ ✗ ✗ ✗

"But what about the sickle?" Maria asked, lifting the finished cassette tape from the machine. "When does it come in?"

"Patience, little one," Professor Appleby chuckled. "All in good time."

Jason placed the next tape into the recorder. The story continued almost immediately.

✗ ✗ ✗ ✗

A cold knot of fear tightened in Naomi's stomach. She and Ruth had found a room to live in, thanks to the kindness of Elimelech's relatives, but they had little food and no man to provide for them. What had she been thinking of, she wondered, to let her daughter-in-law come back to Bethlehem with her? Would they both starve?

She felt a hand on her shoulder and turned to look into Ruth's twinkling eyes. "What's that worried look for?" her daughter-in-law teased. "Today I'm going to follow the reapers in the barley fields. I'll gather as much as I can from what they drop. We won't starve. You'll see!"

As Ruth gave her a quick kiss and left, Naomi shook her head while a smile chased the worry from her eyes. Still she fussed to herself, "Ruth doesn't know what she's getting herself into!"

But Ruth knew. Already she had heard crude and cruel remarks about women from Moab. And she knew that work in the barley fields would be hard.

As she stepped outside the gate of Bethlehem, she looked down at all the golden barley fields basking under bright blue skies. But into which field should she go? Aimlessly her feet led her down the hill, first in one direction, then another.

At last she stood at the edge of a field where whole families worked together. She watched for a moment as the men grasped the stalks of barley with one hand, neatly cut it off with one swing of their curved sickles, and tied it into bundles. Many of the poor and the widows followed after the reapers and picked up the stray kernels that fell to the ground.

Taking a deep breath, she headed into the field. All day she worked. The dry, stiff stubble pricked her fingers. Her back ached. Sweat trickled down her dusty face.

Once, as she stood up straight to ease her back, she spotted an important-looking man inspecting the crop. "The Lord be with you!" he shouted to the laborers, and they all stopped their work to call back to him, "The Lord bless you!" Just then he glanced in Ruth's direction, and she quickly lowered her eyes.

But the man kept staring at her. He wondered if this could be the Moabite girl he had heard so much about—the one who had been so loyal and kind to Naomi. Purposefully he approached his foreman. "Who is that young woman?" he asked, jerking his head in Ruth's direction as she again bent over the barley. Boaz listened carefully, then strode into the field.

"You young men," he barked, "don't bother the Moabite girl! And leave a few stalks for her to pick up. In fact, pull some out of your bundles and leave it in her path."

Then he trudged over to Ruth and spoke to her, lowering his big, booming voice to a kind rumble. "My daughter, stay in my field to glean. Work along with my servant girls. I've made certain that you'll be safe here and gather plenty of grain. When you're thirsty, drink from the water jars the men have filled."

Ruth bowed low before the gentle stranger. "Why are you so good to me—a foreigner?" she asked.

Boaz smiled. "As are most of the people in Bethlehem, Elimelech was a relative of mine, and I've heard of your kindness to his widow. May the Lord richly reward you, and may you find refuge under the wings of the God of Israel!"

Boaz continued to show her many kindnesses. He shared his meal with her, and when at the end of the day she finally threshed out her grain, she had nearly a bushel.

Her feet beat a happy rhythm as she hurried home to Naomi. Bursting through the doorway, she cried, "Look!" and held up her mantle, bulging with grain.

"How did you get so much?" her mother-in-law asked, eyes wide and wondering. Eagerly Ruth told her all about her day, and especially of the kind owner of the field, a man named Boaz.

"Boaz!" Naomi exclaimed. "Why, he's a close relative! Surely the good Lord guided your steps into his field." Her mind began to churn with thoughts she dared not share—not yet, anyway.

One day when Ruth returned from the field with another generous supply of grain, Naomi sat her down and gave her a long and thoughtful look. "Ruth," she began, "in Israel we have a law that says that when a man dies without children, the next of kin must provide children for the dead man by marrying his widow. He must also buy back any of the dead man's property sold to pay debts.

"So—I've been thinking—Boaz could buy back Elimelech's field and marry you to provide children for your dead husband. Now, this is what I want you to do . . ."

Ruth listened, eyes wide, as Naomi outlined a plan that would mean that she, Ruth, would ask Boaz to marry her!

The barley harvest was almost over. Boaz stood at the edge of the flat threshing floor, smiling with satisfaction at the mountain of barley piled on it. Tonight he would again sleep beside the pile of grain so that no one would be tempted to steal it.

Stretching himself on the ground and wrapping himself in his cloak, he soon drifted off to sleep. Suddenly he awoke. All was quiet. The sweet, musty smell of barley filled the darkness.

Then, startled, he felt a movement at his feet. Rearing up, he stared through the gloom at the form of a woman. "Who are you?" he whispered hoarsely.

"I am Ruth," came a soft voice. "Spread the corner of your cloak over me, since you are a close relative." He knew that she had used a phrase that implied a proposal of marriage.

"May the Lord bless you for this kindness!" he exclaimed, admiring the spirit of this girl. Ruth breathed a quick sigh of relief. "And don't worry about anything," he continued. "The whole town knows of your noble character. I understand what you're asking, and I will do all you request.

"However, we have one small problem. You have a male relative closer than I. He must be given first chance to buy back Naomi's property and to marry you. But wait

until morning, and I will take care of everything."

Naomi's eyes shone with happiness as Ruth told her all that had happened the night before. "Boaz is a man of his word!" she declared. "If he said he'll take care of it today, he will!"

Even as she spoke, Boaz sat just inside the town gate in the big open area where everyone gathered to conduct business. Soon Elimelech's other relative came along.

The two men put their heads together and talked long and seriously. At last the other, younger relative said, "Yes, I will buy Naomi's property."

Although Boaz' lips tightened, he spoke as calmly as before when he said, "That will mean, of course, that you will marry Ruth, the Moabite, for she comes with the property."

The other man scowled, paced back and forth, and shook his head. "I can't do that!" he finally exclaimed as a growing crowd gathered around the two men. "If we had children, the property would then go to them, instead of my own family. I can't afford it!" And with that, he yanked off a sandal and handed it to Boaz, a sign that he gave up his property rights to the older man.

Boaz's teeth flashed in a sudden smile. "You are all witnesses!" he boomed happily to the crowd. "I will redeem the land, and I will marry Ruth!"

And in all the land of Israel no happier people could be found than Ruth and Naomi and Boaz. Unless, of course, one counted little Obed, the bright-eyed, black-haired baby boy later born to Ruth and Boaz.

And as Naomi rocked the baby and crooned to it, the women of Bethlehem gathered around her. "Now may we call you Naomi again? The 'pleasant one'? Or do you still want to be called Mara, the 'bitter one'?"

Naomi laughed from embarrassment. "I am no longer bitter," she said softly. "You have said it yourselves—this daughter-in-law of mine is better than seven sons!"

Ruth smiled, full of happiness. But God was to bring her an even greater honor, for someday she would be the great-grandmother of David, Israel's great king, and ancestor of the long-promised Messiah.

ꟷ ꟷ ꟷ ꟷ

"Wow!" Maria gasped as the story came to an end. "Imagine finding your future husband right in the middle of a field. How romantic!"

She sighed and happened to glance in Carl's direction.

"Hey, don't look at me," the boy called, jumping to his feet. "First my mom says I should find a girl with brains; now I hear that some female might be hiding in a cow pasture just waiting to get me to marry her. No way!"

Dr. Morrison laughed. "Calm down, son. You don't have to worry about such things for at least another 30 years. That's when I might let you double-date."

Professor Appleby grinned and nodded. "They grow up

fast, don't they?" Eyeing Stacey, he added, "Too fast sometimes."

The visitor motioned toward the sickle lying on the ground beside the professor. "Mind if I try it?"

"Sure, go ahead," the old man encouraged. "I might even let you handle the original that this is copied from. It's very, very old."

Dr. Morrison picked up the farm tool and walked a few paces into the nearby tall grass. With a wave of his arm he sent the reproduction sickle slicing through the blades with a soft *swishing* sound. Grass toppled and fell.

"Hey, it works!" the man called as another row of stalks tumbled. *Swish. Swish.* The tall grass bent and dropped at his passing, leaving a wide trail through the green growth.

"Seems you've done that kinda work before," Professor Appleby called. "Takes a practiced hand to use a sickle correctly."

"I was raised on a farm about 100 miles from here," the college president said, walking back in the professor's direction. "I've swung a few sickles in my day, but never one made like this." He paused for a long moment. "Sorta gives me a new appreciation of the folks who lived 3,000 years ago. They worked the fields just as I did, sweating under the afternoon sun, waiting for the supper bell to ring. I guess we're not that much different after all."

"Now you sound like my sister," Professor Appleby said with a smile. "She's always telling folk that archaeology proves that civilizations and cultures are more alike than different. If you want to get her ire up, just tell her the Bible is outdated, old-fashioned, or not important for today. Why, she'll look you in the eye and tell you a thing or two. Yup. Sickles may have been replaced by noisy tractors, but the man or woman doing the harvesting, then and now, is very much the same."

Dr. Morrison nodded slowly. Glancing at his son, then at the other children, he said, "I guess the Bible does have something to teach us today."

"Sure," the professor agreed. "And as soon as that college president gets here, I'm going to tell him that very thing."

Morrison grinned. "You do that," he said. "You tell him he should be thankful that people like you and your sister are willing to take the time to bring those old stories to life. And you tell him not to worry about what the community says or thinks on this matter. It's the right thing to do, and he should do it!"

"Hey," Professor Appleby laughed, "maybe you should stick around and tell him yourself."

"Won't be necessary," the visitor said. "I think he'll get the message loud and clear." Turning, he called, "Come on Carl. Let's get home before your mother starts worrying."

As he handed the sickle to the professor, he added, "You're doing a good thing here, my friend. Thanks."

"You're welcome," Professor Appleby nodded politely. "Come anytime. And bring that bright-looking son of yours. Who knows, maybe he and my granddaughter . . ."

"Grandfather!" Stacey gasped.

Professor Appleby winked at his visitor. "Give 'em a few years. Then even a wheat field will seem romantic."

Dr. Morrison smiled and shook the old man's hand. Glancing at the tape recorder, then at his son, he whispered, "Seems some things never change."

As the visitor's car drove away, Stacey walked up to her grandfather and took his hand in hers. "You did good," she said. "Maggie B's going to be proud of you for getting the college president to see things your way."

"Is that who that was?" the old man blinked. "Funny. I thought he was shorter."

Stacey threw her arms around the professor and gave him a big squeeze. "You're the best," she said. "You're the absolute, top-of-the-line, one-of-a-kind best."

BIBLE PEOPLE

```
T O F F T U X G S E M Z L Y Y Q K P E N
H A P R O A P H S D E J F X R A Y V U Q
X Q R M H V J O X C D N H L A I M O A N
S J K M P Z Y K H J J C K N M U B F W O
X B D G A Q T A K Q E O V F V I V Z P L
C U Z E S O R B P L A T J E R C F L N H
E O N J X I N D E W O H V Q K F M G G A
G M T B A J F M A H X I H H J N Z I S M
N O N H E O I I J H F D M B A Z X A G P
D J O N D L G T Q Z Z N J T U F M Z L F
D H I M E U U H M T G A H I D U E C R R
P I L Y G V Q O U D D A W L E A Y B K K
A I I Q N X X U K A N K N L C Z D D A X
G M H S J E S U S A Y X X H G R J O H N
W P C H J A Y O E U H T U R P K K I U X
E R L T A N O L L T M O Z L N E B Y I F
P I T H I J W G E J B Y A A I S S R T O
W E O G T D D I V A D S O B R V S O O S
K L I A G I B A O C P P B A V D X U J F
B H H F U W X K Z N Q Z H N R P I H G V
```

ABIGAIL	JOHN	NATHANAEL
BOAZ	JOSEPH	ORPAH
CHILION	MAHLON	RUTH
DAVID	MARY	SAMUEL
ELIMELECH	NABAL	ZECHARIAH
JESUS	NAOMI	

Water, Water Anywhere?

Unlike Mesopotamia, with its Tigris and Euphrates rivers and Egypt with its Nile, Palestine has few permanent rivers. Farmers couldn't use them to irrigate their crops. In ancient times the Israelites had to depend completely upon rainfall to grow their food.

Unfortunately, rain does not fall year-round in the Holy Land. The cities of London and Jerusalem both receive about the same amount of rainfall, but while it rains every few days in London, most of the rain in Jerusalem comes only in heavy downpours during a short period of a few weeks.

The Holy Land has a wet season and a dry season. The dry season is regular, starting about June 15 and ending about September 15. The only moisture the land receives then is dew. The first torrential rains of the unpredictable wet season may start as early as October or as late as December. The winter storms can follow each other in a regular pattern, or long periods can occur between them. Heavy storms create flash floods, but the water quickly runs away and does not soak into the hard, rocky soil to feed the wells and springs.

If the land goes too long without the winter rainstorms or the rain comes at the wrong time, seeds will not germinate, and crops will fail. (During the six-week periods between the wet and dry seasons there will usually be some light showers, but not enough to really water the soil.)

Sometimes rain will fall heavily in one spot, but it will remain dry only a few miles away. This may be why Bethlehem in the time of Naomi had famine while Moab, only 30 miles away, had rainfall and thus food.* The mountains block the rainfall as it tries to move inland. Since 1859 Jerusalem, on top of the mountains running north-south through Israel, has received an average of 26 inches of rainfall each year. Jericho, less than 20 miles farther east and below the mountains, averages only 5.5 inches.

More rainfall falls in the north than the south. Galilee gets heavy rainfall and is green much of the year, while the south or Negev is desert and is green only during the winter. For each mile one travels south toward Bethlehem, the average rainfall drops one inch.

More rain falls on the western slope of a hill, and evaporation is greater on the southern slopes. As a result the land is greener in winter and vegetation greater all through the year on the western and northern sides of a hill than on the southern and eastern.

All these things make getting enough water a constant problem to the people of the Holy Land.

The Israelites tried to build their villages and cities near springs, such as the famous Gihon spring at Jerusalem. But there were not enough springs to go around, especially in the hilly and desert country, nor were they always dependable. Wells provided water elsewhere, but they dry up near the end of summer. Thus people had to find other ways of collecting and storing water when it did come during the rainy season.

To catch and hold the unpredictable rainwater, people carved cisterns out of the rocky ground. Cisterns are large human-made caves that the Israelite settlers dug into the ground to collect the rainwater. Cisterns are shaped like bottles or pears, with an opening or neck just wide enough for the man digging it to climb down through. This reduces the amount of water that will evaporate from it.

But once the cistern has been dug down a few feet, it begins to widen out. Cisterns could be as big as rooms or even whole buildings. Plaster on the walls kept the water from leaking away into the porous limestone. Drains from roofs, courtyards, streets, and even open spaces of land channeled the heavy downpours to the cisterns. During New Testament times the Romans built aqueducts to bring water

10 miles to fill one large cistern. It was 43 feet deep and could hold more than 2 million gallons. (In addition they built an aqueduct to bring water from the hills to the seaport of Caesarea.)

Stone or wooden covers over the entrance kept people and animals from falling in. People had to make sure that sewage or dead animals did not contaminate the water as it flowed into the cistern and cause those who drank it to get sick. Some cisterns had crude filters at their mouths to trap debris. Pieces of pottery, coins, bits of jewelry, and even whole skeletons found in the cisterns tell us that people did not clean them very often.

Ancient cisterns honeycomb the hills of Israel. Most homes had their own cisterns. Many towns and cities had large public ones. Ancient Jerusalem had many cisterns in spite of the fact that it had abundant springwater. Such cisterns stored rainwater for those times when the winter rains did not come, or when enemy armies cut off a town or city from the regular wells and springs.

When the cisterns were dry, people used them for storage or even as temporary dungeons. Joseph and Jeremiah were imprisoned in unused or nearly dry cisterns. A cistern below the Church of St. Peter in Jerusalem had a guard room dug for it when it was used as a prison.

_____

*Scholars have suggested still another reason Moab may have had food when Bethlehem did not. When the British ruled Palestine after World War I, they kept records of the rainfall. Extremely hot weather often occurs during times of drought. When it got very hot, the British noticed, more water evaporated from the Dead Sea. It formed clouds that drifted east toward the land of Jordan. As the clouds rose over the mountains east of the Dead Sea, they would drop their moisture as rain on what had once been the ancient land of Moab. The rainfall kept the crops growing there, and the people had food.

⑤

A Proper Name

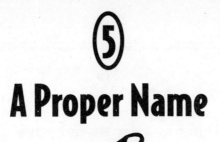

Miss Baker scratched her head and sighed. "I don't know, Professor," she said. "I think it looked better over by the Israelite pottery collection."

Professor Appleby nodded and maneuvered a bucket-shaped stone container across the den floor, huffing and puffing with the exertion. "Why didn't the Egyptians use wristwatches like normal people?" he moaned.

"What exactly is that thing?" Miss Baker asked.

The professor paused to wipe sweat from his brow. "Maggie B says it's a reproduction of a water clock. Found the original while digging at Lachish, a fortress city in Judah. She said Isaiah foretold that city's destruction by Assyrian invaders. Guess they missed this."

"How's it work?" the woman wanted to know.

"Well, this hole in the bottom is supposed to let water out at a certain rate. You fill the bucket to this mark, then wait. When the water level hits the next mark down, so much time has passed. All these positions on the scale indicate that a portion of the day has gone by."

Miss Baker nodded. "I guess clocks back then didn't go tick, tick, tick. They went drip, drip, drip."

"And you didn't *wind* them, you *filled* them," the professor laughed.

"I'll just stick with my digital timepiece, if it's all right with you," she chuckled. "It doesn't tick, drip, fill up, or wind down. It just sits there and blinks."

With a final puff Professor Appleby wrestled the heavy stone bucket-clock into position by a collection of eating utensils and pottery bowls. "There," he said with a satisfied sigh. "Now everyone can tell when it's time to eat."

Miss Baker flopped down in a nearby chair. "I think

we're making some progress," she announced wearily. "We've got pre-literate over there by the door, the Fertile Crescent objects next to it. The Patriarchal Period material is by the window. Egyptian artifacts and reproductions are sitting by the fireplace, and the Canaan collection is resting up on those less-than-adequate shelves. Now we've just got to figure out where to put the Persian and Jerusalem assortments. Any ideas?"

Professor Appleby sank down beside the woman. "I never knew just how much variety Maggie B has in her collection. Look at all this stuff! And I must say it was kind of a shock when the college board decided that not only is the town going to have a museum of antiquity, but it's going to be started here in my own house!"

"You have the perfect place for it," Miss Baker smiled. "Besides, this way we won't have to move everything."

"But I'm not sure this one room will be enough. We don't want folks to see piles of artifacts or heaps of strange-looking gizmos lying around without some kind of order to them."

"Patience," Miss Baker said with a smile. "We're just getting things organized into time periods. Then we can make labels and set up displays. Don't want to get a Greek warrior statue mixed up with a Phoenician fertility goddess. No telling what would happen."

The professor shook his head. "Another shipment's coming in this afternoon. Got a call from the freight people yesterday. Maggie B sent a whole boat."

"A boat?"

"Yup. Made out of reeds. She said she built it herself. I wouldn't have been surprised if she had tried to sail it all the way from Egypt."

"Well, we'd better figure out where we're going to put it," the woman laughed.

"Put what?" a young voice called from the doorway as Stacey and her two friends entered the room. Just behind them strode Carl, his face reflecting the excitement they were all feeling at seeing the progress being made in the professor's large den.

"My dad wants to know how it's coming," the boy announced.

Miss Baker shook her head. "Slowly. We've been at it for a week, and all we have to show for our efforts are big piles and little piles. And Maggie B is always sending new stuff. We can hardly keep up."

"Looks . . . organized," Stacey chuckled, examining a vase with strange figures carved into it. "Where'd this come from?"

"Beirut," the professor said. "Some friend of Maggie B's found it in his backyard while he was digging for a new cistern."

"Is it old?" Stacey asked.

"Not really, as an archaeologist would judge time. But it's interesting. The man thought Maggie B might like it for her collection."

Carl eyed the tape recorder resting on the small end table by the door. "Got any new tapes?"

"Sure do," Professor Appleby grinned. "Came this morning. They're out in the foyer on the umbrella stand. Why don't you guys find a spot in the kitchen and give them a listen? Help yourself to the fruit juice in the refrigerator. Oh, and don't drink the blue stuff in the glass jar. I should know what it is, but I don't remember."

"OK," Stacey called as she and the others headed out into the foyer. "Kitchen . . . listen . . . no blue stuff. Got it."

The professor smiled and glanced over at his hardworking companion. "Were we ever that young?" he asked.

"I think so," Miss Baker giggled. "A very, very long time ago."

With a laugh the two turned to the task at hand.

Maria frowned at the words scrawled across the label of the first new tape. "Nabal and A . . . bi . . . gail. Whew. Maggie B's writing is worse than mine. That's saying a lot."

"Who's Nabal and Abigail?" Jason asked, pulling up a chair and seating himself at the shiny-topped table.

"Sounds like a couple lawyers," Stacey chuckled.

"I guess the only way we'll find out is to listen to the tape," Carl said, plugging in the recorder and flipping open the little door on top of the machine. "You ready?"

"Ready!" came the happy reply.

✂ ✂ ✂ ✂

David's glance wandered over his band of men. Once strangers, runaways from Saul and his government, they had become trusted friends. And they had grown into an efficient little army, protecting Israel's borders, defending shepherds and farmers from desert raiders. More recently they had mourned with him at the death of the old prophet Samuel.

Now, once again, they faced hunger. He looked into their trusting faces. "What's the plan, chief?" a grizzled old warrior questioned.

David had an answer. "Nabal, the rich farmer and landowner, is shearing his sheep at Carmel. I'll send 10 of the younger fellows there to ask him for food."

The old man grinned, revealing a gap where three front teeth were missing. "That's it!" he chuckled. "He owes us plenty of favors for all the times we protected his shepherds and flocks."

Beckoning to 10 of his young friends, David told them exactly what to say to Nabal.

A feeling of celebration hung over the fields as the shepherds sheared the sheep. Loud laughter, rowdy songs, and a constant chorus of bleats and baas drowned out the sounds of approaching footsteps. As soon as the shearing was done and the wool sold, the shepherds would be paid, so it was a festive time of year. David's men paused as they approached the noisy scene.

The wealthy landowner Nabal stood with arms folded across his chest. His sharp little eyes darted here and there, watching everything. Did that shearer miss a tuft of wool? He bellowed a rebuke. Was that man slowing down? "Hurry up! What do you think I pay you for?"

But while he scowled and bellowed, his heart beat a greedy little rhythm. This year he had more sheep and goats than ever before—a thousand goats and three thousand sheep! He was rich—the richest man around!

Then out of the corner of his eye he saw some strangers approaching. They were armed like bandits, and his heart thumped a different rhythm. Were they part of one of those dreadful tribes of looters from the desert? But no, they had an honest look about them. He eyed them narrowly as they came closer.

The men remembered exactly what David had told them to say. Bowing low before Nabal, and smiling pleasantly, they repeated, "We greet you in the name of David, the son of Jesse! Long life to you, and good health to your household!"

"Hmph!" Nabal grunted, immediately on guard. *They probably want something from me,* he grumbled to himself.

But David's men continued to speak respectfully. "David has told us to say that he has heard of your sheep-shearing and celebration. We have protected your shepherds and your flocks. In all the time we've been nearby, you've not lost a sheep, a goat, or even a blanket.

"So now your son David requests that at this happy time you share whatever you have on hand with us."

Nabal scowled. He didn't want to give away anything, even though it was a common practice to share with one's protectors. He didn't care if David did call himself his "son" in the most respectful way possible. And it meant nothing to him that David had protected his flocks. He wanted everything for himself.

Turning on the waiting men, he snarled, "And who is David, and who is Jesse, that I should share my goods? Why should I take my bread and water and give it to men who suddenly arrive from nowhere?

"The answer is no. No, no, no!"

Shocked into silence by the man's rudeness, not to mention his stinginess, the little group backed away from Nabal, bowed again, then took to their heels.

David's face flushed a dark, angry red as he listened to their report. His eyes flashed dangerously. "I swear I'll not leave one male among his household alive!" he stormed. "Strap on your swords!"

Quietly the men obeyed. Never had they seen David so angry or so reckless. He hadn't even stopped to ask God if he was doing the right thing.

From the rooftop of her home that evening Abigail, Nabal's wife, breathed deeply of the cool air. Valleys, filled with purple shadows, nestled against the soft brown of the hills. She felt at peace.

Suddenly a servant, panting loudly, scrambled onto the rooftop. Abigail's eyes filled with concern. "You seem troubled," she smiled gently, noting his frightened expression.

"Oh, mistress," he exclaimed, "wait until you hear what the master has done!" Quickly he told her of Nabal's selfish, foolish actions in the field that day. "How could he do that after David's men protected us like a strong wall?" he wailed. "They deserve great generosity. Now the master's actions may cost us all our lives!"

Abigail sighed. *Again?* she thought. Would her selfish husband never learn? But her first concern was for the frightened servant. "Don't worry," she smiled, "I'll take care of it."

The servant bowed. Already he felt better. *If only my master would behave more like my beautiful mistress!* he thought.

Abigail flew into action. Of all the foolish things her husband had done, this was by far the most dangerous. Rousing her servants, she issued soft, clear orders.

Soon delicious odors wafted from the cooking area of the courtyard. Soon every corner overflowed with raisin cakes, bulging wineskins, loaves of flat, round bread, and bunches of dried figs. Servants tied up odd-shaped packages of mutton from five fat sheep. And Abigail poured a bushel of her best roasted grain into leather pouches.

In the pale light of morning a quiet little caravan started down the winding path toward Carmel. Sleepy donkeys with half-closed eyes plodded along, carrying all the food on their backs. Servants shuffled along beside them. And at the very end of the caravan, riding on a donkey, sat Abigail.

If I head toward Carmel, she thought, *I should meet David and his men. And with God's help I'll be able to stop him before he attacks!*

Gaining the crest of a hill, Abigail suddenly stared straight ahead. David and his men swarmed over the hill facing her. His angry words echoed in the air: ". . . and to think of all the times we saved that man's flocks! By this time tomorrow he and his household will all be dead!"

Abigail's servants started to retreat from fear, but she whispered a quick prayer and slipped off her donkey, showing her respect for the handsome leader of the band.

Suddenly David's angry words died on his lips as he watched, fascinated. Even at a distance this woman sparkled like a jewel on the dusty road. Slowly she descended the hill.

He raced down toward her. At last they met in a little valley. Abigail's servants and David's men hardly breathed. What was this woman about to do?

Abigail bowed low, her hair, shiny and black as a raven's wing, brushing David's feet. Curious, spellbound, he invited her to rise. With one smooth motion she stood and looked full into his face.

Stunned by the intensity of Abigail's dark eyes and the seriousness of her mouth, David caught his breath. Then she began to speak.

"I am Abigail, wife of Nabal," she began. "Place the blame for this trouble on me. My husband, Nabal, can't be

blamed, for he is a foolish man, and does foolish things."
She gave a short little laugh. "What else can you expect of
a man named 'Fool'?"

David felt his admiration for her growing with her every
word. To think that she would take the blame for her husband's actions!

But Abigail hurried on. "I know that a man as big-
hearted as you could not possibly take notice of someone so
far beneath him as Nabal," she suggested.

Firmly but gently she added, "And my lord will surely
keep himself from the evil of shedding the blood of fellow
Israelites."

At last she declared, her shining eyes never leaving his
face, "The Lord has kept you from bloodshed."

David listened, confused and amazed by Abigail's wisdom. He didn't remember deciding not to take revenge on
Nabal, but somehow he knew he had.

But she hadn't finished. "May the Lord who has kept
you from bloodshed and from doing something only God
has a right to do protect you from all your enemies. May
He keep you from wrongdoing all the days of your life, so
that your reign will last forever!"

Suddenly his conscience hurt. She had just reminded him
that he was God's anointed, chosen to be Israel's next king.
He had been so close to doing something that would have
made all Israel wonder if he was worthy of being their king.

And worst of all, he had been ready to do things his
own way, not God's.

Now Abigail turned to her servants and with a few soft-
spoken orders sent them scurrying to unload the donkeys.
David felt a lump in his throat as Abigail offered his hungry men enough food for a banquet. Nabal's wife was as
kind and generous as her husband was mean and miserly.

At last finding his tongue, David thanked her again and
again, not only for her gifts but for her wisdom in turning
him away from wrongdoing.

His reward was a smile so brilliant he felt the sun had just come out at midnight. Deep in thought, he watched her ride away until she was out of sight.

Now Abigail had one more thing to do. She must find Nabal and tell him what had happened.

But when she finally found her husband, he was drunk. He and his servants sprawled at a banquet table, red wine staining their robes. Disgusted, she turned away.

But the next morning she shook him until his bleary eyes focused on her. "What? What? Whadya want?" he growled.

"Listen to me!" she commanded, her dark eyes flashing. "The Lord has spared your life and the lives of every man in your household!" Quickly she told him the whole story.

But when she came to the part about giving away five sheep, 200 loaves of bread, and all the other food, his eyes popped out of his head, blood pounded in his ears, and he fell back on his bed like a rock. From that moment on, he was unable to move.

Ten days later Nabal died.

Hearing what had happened, David immediately thought of Abigail. He wanted this beautiful, wise, and good woman to be his wife.

And Abigail, happy and willing, soon joined him and his band of outlaws.

� ✗ ✗ ✗

"Man, that was close!" Jason breathed when the story ended. "Old Nabal and his men were about to be mincemeat. That Abigail was one brave lady."

"All women are brave," Maria retorted.

"Yeah, right," Jason laughed.

"They are!" Stacey pressed. "Take my mom. She's brave. She's editor of the town paper, works hard all day, and earns enough money for us to live on. Sometimes she has to go out and get stories from the police department and the mayor's office. I've seen her do interviews with people who aren't very nice at all. She doesn't back down an inch. My mom gets her story no matter what it takes."

"Yeah," Maria joined in. "And my mom and dad brought me all the way from Mexico City. Took us three months. Dad says Mom was very brave to make the journey. Wasn't easy, believe me."

"All right, all right!" Jason cried, lifting his hands. "I guess women can be just as brave as men."

Carl laughed. "Well, my dad said Miss Baker really put up a fight to have the museum started here in Professor Appleby's house. He said she did some pretty heavy convincing. But I'm glad she did. As soon as everything's up and running, they're going to let other kids come out here to listen to the tapes with us. It's going to be great!"

"Yeah," Stacey interjected. "But first they gotta get some work done on the house so the college can use part of it for the museum and listening room. Mom said Chief Nelson from the fire station came out here to inspect the place. He took one look and started laughing. Guess they got to do some renovation. But Grandfather said it won't take more than a few months to get everything in order. Then the fun will really begin."

"Imagine," Maria said, looking off into space. "We're going to have our own museum of antiquity right here in our town. And *we're* going to help fix it up. I know where I'll be spending my summer."

"Me too," the others chorused.

"Hey, we got to think of a name for it," Jason said.

Stacey blinked. "You're right. A proper museum has to have a proper name."

The room fell silent as four hands rubbed four chins. "This isn't going to be easy," Carl said. "It's gotta be special, really special."

"Well," Jason sighed, reaching for the other cassette tape lying on the table, "why don't we think about it while we listen to Maggie B's next story? She wrote 'Wedding at

Cana' on the label."

"That figures," Carl moaned. "First we have some woman finding the man of her dreams in a field, then another lady getting her good-for-nothing husband off the hook with David. She later joins up with him after her husband conks off. And now here's a wedding story. Sure is a lot of mushy stuff in the Bible."

Stacey grinned. "Love is nice, and I like it."

"Stay away from me," Carl said, moving his chair to the far side of the table.

The girl shook her head. Turning to Maria, she said, "Men. They're impossible."

"Yeah," Maria agreed, lifting her nose into the air. With a flourish the girl swished her hand back and forth, then settled her index finger on the play button of the tape recorder.

Maggie B's voice filled the cozy kitchen once again.

✗ ✗ ✗ ✗

Abbie and Abner raced through the little streets of Cana, a little town not far from Nazareth. Brown eyes dancing, cheeks glowing, they ran past tiny shops where farmers sold sweet-smelling fruit. They sped past beggars, lame or blind, past the well in the center of the village where a few women lingered, and finally to their stone house.

Mother bent over a steaming pot in the courtyard. "Something sure smells good!" Abner announced hopefully. She glanced up at him. "It's your favorite, red lentil stew," she smiled.

But her smile faded as she looked at Abbie. "And where was my daughter when it was time to peel the onions and chop the garlic?" she scolded.

The girl gazed miserably at her brown toes peeking through her sandals. "I, uh, was listening to some people talk, and I, uh, guess I forgot!" she stammered.

Mother stifled a smile. "And what did these people have

to say that was so interesting?" she asked.

"They were talking about a man called Jesus, and some-one named Nathanael said He's the Messiah!"

Mother paused, forgetting to stir the stew. "I've seen this Jesus," she spoke softly. "I was in the crowd at the Jordan River when John, son of Zechariah, baptized Him. And there does seem something quite special about Him. But how could He be the Messiah? Everyone knows He's the son of Mary, and of Joseph the carpenter."

Abbie decided to change the subject. "Mother, we're going to the wedding of Nathan and Hodiah, aren't we?"

"Yes, Abbie, we'll all go. As a matter of fact, I promised to help Mary of Nazareth with the food. She's this Jesus' mother. Probably He will be there. You, Abigail, may help me if you think you can remember to be around when you're supposed to!"

But Abbie hardly heard her mother's words. Nathan's and Hodiah's wedding was almost here! And Abbie loved weddings. Her mind wandered back three years before to the time Nathan and Hodiah had become engaged. Hodiah had been about 12 and Nathan 14.

After Nathan's and Hodiah's fathers had decided that their children would marry, Nathan's father had given some money, a bride-price, to Hodiah's father. The young couple had exchanged presents. Then Hodiah had slipped a veil over her face and worn it ever since, so that no other young man would see how pretty she was.

Abbie sighed. Someday her father would pick out a hus-band for her. She hoped he would be good and kind like her father—and handsome like Nathan!

But soon there would be a wedding—seven whole days of music and dancing and games and riddles! Tables would overflow with delicious cakes and breads. The women of Cana had ground extra wheat and barley and had made a thick, rich syrup from the juice of grapes and dates. They had gathered almonds and pistachios.

Finally they would mix all the ingredients together, and out of the clay ovens would come delicious raisin cakes and fig cakes and nut breads. Kindhearted farmers would donate a precious sheep or goat for the wedding feast, and many a chicken would find its way to the cooking pot.

The harvest of fruit had ended, but purple stains on Abbie's feet and the hem of her dress still reminded her of joyfully stamping the fragrant grapes. She knew there would be plenty of new wine to wash down all that food!

Finally the wedding day arrived. Everyone waited for evening. At last the red sun slid behind Mount Carmel, purple in the distance, and the green hills of Galilee faded into soft, rosy shadows. Soon the bridegroom would appear.

Abbie and Abner dashed into the street, joining their friends who already jammed the dusty roads. Still others sat on the flat roofs of their houses, watching for the bridegroom. Carrying torches, people laughed, and sang, and danced. Abbie shook her tambourine in the air with all her might.

From other nearby towns—Nazareth, Magdala, Tiberias—people streamed into Cana. Eagerly they waited for the bridegroom.

Suddenly a shout went up. "Here he comes!" And the bridegroom appeared, riding high on a fancy litter, a kind of couch carried by his friends. He wore a smile that set his whole face aglow. And as he nodded his head in greeting to his friends, his diadem, like a crown for a king, shone in the torchlight.

"To the bride's house! To the bride's house!" Like a wave on the Sea of Galilee, the crowd surged down the street, dancing and singing. Above them the flaming torches danced and sparkled as if they too were celebrating.

At last they reached Hodiah's home. Carried on a litter, and with her own happy attendants, the bride joined her husband-to-be.

Abbie gasped when she saw Hodiah's wedding clothes. Bright, beautiful colors—red, yellow, and green—swirled around her, and she sparkled with jewels. A crown of coins, her wedding gift from Nathan, nestled in her dark and flowing hair. Over her face hung a heavy veil.

Everyone watched as her attendants lifted her from her own litter to Nathan's. Like a king and queen they rode above the crowd, back to the home of the bridegroom.

People clapped their hands and sang of the beauty of the bride, the bravery of the groom. Some scattered nuts and roasted grain before the couple while others poured oil, wine, and perfume onto the dusty road. Now, they felt sure, the young bride and her husband would have a home filled with happiness and children.

Back at Nathan's house once more, Abbie and Abner squeezed in with Mother and Father. Suddenly they spotted a group of young men talking and laughing together. Among them they recognized the man called Nathanael.

But something about another young man, the One in the center of the group, caught their attention, and held it. Abbie tried to figure out what was different about Him. He spoke with a Galilean accent. But so did the others. He wore one of the wedding garments that Nathan had passed out to the guests. But the others did too. Nothing about Him was unusual. Yet *something* about Him was most unusual!

Abbie knew only that His laugh seemed warmer, His eyes kinder, than those of anyone else she had ever known. Abner gazed at the man's strong, work-hardened hands, and wondered how they could still seem so gentle.

The children stared at each other. *This must be Jesus!* Suddenly He saw them, too. White teeth flashed in a beautiful smile, and warm eyes held them in a look that was like a hug.

But Mother hurried them along. They heard the parents of the groom pronounce a blessing on Nathan and Hodiah as they sat under a colorful canopy. Now the couple was married!

Suddenly servants sprang into action, bringing water

to the guests. Abbie and Abner washed themselves just as others did. The guests hurried to lie down on the couches around the long table, propping themselves on one elbow.

Not everyone could eat at the same time, so Abbie scampered after Mother to help with the food. They found Mary, the mother of Jesus, heaping bread onto a tray.

The feast went on until long past midnight. Finally the happy people returned to their homes, knowing that tomorrow they would have clothes to mend, trees to prune, land to plow. But tomorrow evening there would again be feasting and celebration.

Night after night the feast continued. The smiling bride now appeared without her veil. The bridegroom mingled with his friends, telling riddles, eating and drinking, singing, reciting poetry. And the guests showered Nathan and Hodiah with presents.

One evening Abbie again went with Mother to ask Mary if she needed help. But they found Mary talking with the servants. As they drew near, they could see the servants waving their hands in an excited, worried way. And Mary looked upset.

Abbie edged closer so she could hear. "Are you sure there is no more wine?" Mary asked.

No more wine! Oh, how embarrassing! The guests would think Nathan was not a good host. How could this have happened?

Suddenly Mary stood very straight, and said, "Please bring my Son Jesus to me." The servants hurried away.

Abbie watched closely as Jesus entered the room. Mary stared at her Son. How could He have changed so in the weeks since she had last seen Him, she wondered. He looked thinner. But more than that, His face bore the marks of one who had suffered.

"My Son," she said, "there is no more wine."

Jesus answered softly, with just a hint of a smile, "Dear

woman, why have you come to Me with this problem? My time has not yet come."

Mary didn't even answer Him. It seemed to Abbie that she simply trusted Jesus to help her when she had a problem. She had told Him her troubles, so now she could forget them.

Turning to the servants, she directed, "Do whatever He tells you to!" Then, as if putting the whole matter out of her mind, she asked Abbie's mother, "Would you like to help me with the trays now?"

But Abbie watched Jesus. He smiled in His mother's direction, then turned to the servants and instructed, "Fill those jars with water." Abbie noticed the six stone water jars standing in the sunlight against the wall. Kept there for ceremonial washing, each one could hold up to 30 gallons.

The servants poured clear, sparkling water into the first jar, into the second, and finally into all six jars. Then, to Abbie's surprise, Jesus said, "Now take some out and give it to the master of the feast."

Why would Jesus tell the servants to take water to the master of the feast? Abbie wondered. The guests needed wine, not water!

And where was Abner? He had to see this! Quick as a sparrow, Abbie darted about until she found him. "Hurry! Come see what happens when they give *water* to the master of the feast!" she told her brother.

Standing in the corner, they watched as the servants dipped into the water and began to pour it into the master's cup. But as it poured, something happened. Abbie's and Abner's eyes grew big and round. The clear water took on the rich, dark red color of wine!

The master of the feast tasted it. His eyes lit up and he smiled. Then he called Nathan and said, "I don't understand what you're doing, Nathan! Bridegrooms always serve their best wine first, but you have saved the best until almost the end of the feast. Where did you get such delicious wine?"

Nathan didn't know what to say, but the servants did. Quickly they told what had happened.

Soon everyone was talking about the water that had been turned into wine. "It's a miracle!" they gasped. And everyone echoed the words. "It's a miracle! It's a miracle!"

The people grew more and more excited. "Where is He?" they asked. "Where is the miracle worker, the man called Jesus?"

But while everyone was discussing the wonderful miracle of the wine, Jesus had quietly disappeared. Away from the crowd, He prayed, "Thank You, Father, for showing Me the way to begin My ministry."

Abbie lay in bed that night while flaming torches and flashing diadems seemed to dance behind her closed eyelids. She heard the rattle of tambourines and the sweet notes of flutes and harps. And she saw water pouring from a jug, but it wasn't water, it was wine . . . water, wine, water, wine . . .

Then she saw a face, the kindest ever. She heard Jesus' warm and wonderful laughter.

Just then her mother peeked in at her. *The child is smiling in her sleep,* Mother thought. *She must be dreaming!*

And Abbie was dreaming—of Jesus' first miracle, the miracle of the wine.

❈ ❈ ❈ ❈

A TURN OF EVENTS

J esus' first miracle at the wedding turned a potentially embarrassing situation back into the happy occasion it was intended to be. Below are letters that should form a phrase. Each letter, however, is one letter off. It is either the letter before or the letter after the correct letter in the alphabet. Figure out whether to go up one or down one, and turn this senseless phrase into a miraculous act.

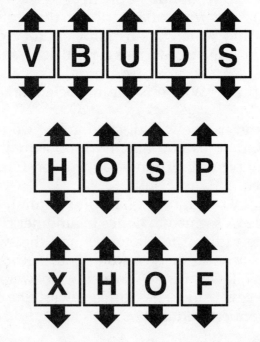

"I've got it!" Stacey called, jumping to her feet.

"Got what?" Maria asked.

"The name for the new museum."

"Didn't you even listen to the story?"

"Every word. I can do two things at once. Can't you?"

Maria smiled. "But I was too busy trying to figure out how Jesus did that water-to-wine thing."

"Yeah," Carl joined in. "How *did* He do that?"

"Maybe he used magic," Jason offered.

"Magic? No way," Maria countered. "After all, if God can create the world by just saying a few words, turning water to wine would be a piece of cake for Him."

"Hey," Stacey whined, "doesn't anyone want to know the name I came up with?"

"Oh yeah, sorry," Maria said. "What's this wonderful name you figured out when you were supposed to be listening to Maggie B's story?"

"Well, picture this," Stacey said, pointing to a spot above the kitchen door. "There's this great big sign outside on the porch. In big, golden letters carved in a wide slab of stone, it says, 'Welcome to Professor Appleby's Museum of Really Old Stuff.'" She looked about the room. "Catchy, huh?"

"I like it," Maria nodded.

"Sounds mysterious," Jason said.

"Maybe the water tasted like wine to begin with," Carl sighed.

"*Carl!*" the others groaned. "The name? What do you think of Stacey's name for the museum?"

"Really Old Stuff, eh?"

"Yeah," Stacey smiled. "People will read that and say to themselves, 'What really old stuff?' Then they'll come inside to find out."

"I don't know," Carl said, shaking his head slowly from side to side. "Maybe we'd better ask the professor."

The four friends filed from the kitchen and hurried out into the foyer. Entering the den, they found Professor

Appleby and Miss Baker standing before a mural depicting an ancient battle scene.

"Hey, Grandfather," Stacey called, "we want to ask you something."

"What is it?"

Stacey cleared her throat. "We decided this place needs a name. But it can't be just any old name like 'The College Foundation of Important Studies' or something awful like that."

"I see," the professor grinned. "And you've come up with just the right title for my little abode in the woods?"

"Yup," Stacey said, lifting her chin. "How about 'Professor Appleby's Museum of Really Old Stuff'?"

Miss Baker's eyelids rose as she pursed her lips. "I think that says it all, don't you agree, Professor?"

The old man nodded slowly. "You're right. 'Professor Appleby,' that's me. 'Museum,' that's what we're putting together. 'Really Old Stuff' certainly describes what's going to be displayed." He turned to his granddaughter. "It's a wonderful name."

He frowned. "Now, the college people may decide to give it some awful, fancy title. But we won't care. We'll know what the real name is, won't we? And whenever we discuss the museum, we'll use its proper name. Deal?"

"Deal!" the children shouted.

"But before we can call it anything, we've got to get this place in order. Miss Baker and I have finally figured out what should be done. Now we just need some willing hands and strong arms to help out. How 'bout it, guys? You ready to get busy and make Maggie B's dream come true?"

"Let's do it!" everyone cheered.

Stacey, Maria, Jason, and Carl stood in line to get instructions from Miss Baker. Much work lay ahead. But the young people didn't mind. Dreams aren't always easy to fulfill. They'd learned that lesson from the many adventures recorded on the cassette tapes. But they were also learning that if you want something badly enough and are willing to work hard for it, anything is possible—even a museum in an old mansion where a kindly professor lived, and where children could hear Bible stories from the lips of Maggie B.

BIBLE PLACES

```
S L I D P V H X I E X Y A E E U P K M L
A Y Q U S A C Z C A R M E L T N Z J O W
I J C W N N Y J E R U S A L E M B E N U
A F H A R A N W B K V L I Z F C Y C M R
V S M Y E F V D D A K O E P A X J B H R
N P A P B Z Y Q L M D G H P V K O F E F
L A P R V D C A E C Y C E B Y U R H C A
D B A R M A D H X P K R B E W C D Q A D
D E Z N R G E K T V N M R D F Y A B N L
Q G O H A L N Y U A S V O A Q Y N M A Q
K E F M H C Y T U S B U N I R J F J C N
C N I T J E S M U H H R T M L F Z C U G
F C E Z W G D N T A A J F A H H G N C W
Q B C U U Q F E F H M U B T P S F B M V
U R E K B H R K R O T D K O Y I J Y G X
W W H L E A T K A U G A O P A H X T L J
Z N V G Z O A B N E H H G O C C M X D W
T G C A Z Q U S P Q P D P S Y A C X L V
S H N B A Y I O E H D J C E S L A O P R
X M C K F S F S C H C O V M L E N E D E
```

BETHLEHEM	EGYPT	LACHISH
CANA	HARAN	MAGDALA
CANAAN	HEBRON	MESOPOTAMIA
CAPERNAUM	JERUSALEM	MOAB
CARMEL	JORDAN	NAZARETH
EDEN	JUDAH	NEGEB

ANSWER KEYS FOR PUZZLES

OUT ON A LIMB, P. 23

PIECING IT TOGETHER, P. 72

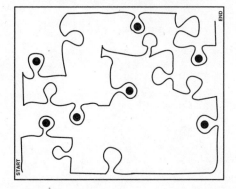

BIBLE PEOPLE, P. 47

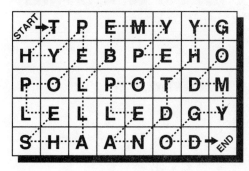

TRACE OF LOYALTY, P. 91

BIBLE PEOPLE, P. 100

```
T O F F T U X G S E M Z L Y Y Q K P E N
H A P R O A P H S D E J F X R A Y V U Q
X Q R M H V J O X C D N H L A I M O A H
S J K M P Z Y K H J J C K N M U B F W O
X B D G A Q I X K Q E O V F V I V Z P L
C U Z E S O R B P L A T J E R C F L N H
E O N J X I N D E W O H V Q K F M G G A
G M T B A J F M A H X I H H J N Z I E M
N O D H E O I I J H F D M B A Z X A G P
D J O N D E G I Q Z Z N J U F M Z L F
D H M E U U H M I G A H I D D E C R R
P I L Y G V Q O U D D A W L E A Y B K K
A I Q N X X U K A N K N Z C Z D D A X
G M H S J E S U S X Y X X H G R J O H N
W P C H J A Y O E U H T U R X K X I U X
E R L I A N O L L I M O Z L N F B Y I F
P I T H I J W G E J B Y A A I S R R I O
W E O G T D D I V A D S O B R V S O O S
K L I A G I B A O C P P B A V D X U F
B H H F U W X K Z N Q Z H R P I H G V
```

A TURN OF EVENTS, P. 122
Water Into Wine

BIBLE PLACES, P. 126

```
S L I D P V H X I E X Y A E E U P K M L
A Y Q U S A C Z C A R M E L T N Z J O W
I J C W N N Y J E R U S A L E M B E N U
A F H A R A N W B K V L I Z F C Y C M K
V S M Y E F V D D A K O E P A X B H R
N P A P B Z Y Q I M D G H V K O F E F
L A P R V D C A E C Y C E B Y U R H C A
D B A R M A D H X E K B E W C D Q A D
D E Z H R G E K I V N M R D F Y A B N L
Q G O H E N Y U A S V O A Q Y N M A Q
K E F M H C Y I U S B U N R J F J C N
C N I J E S M U H H R T M L F Z C U G
F C E Z W G D N T A A F A H H G N C W
Q B C U U Q F E F H M U B T P S F B M V
U R E K B H R K R O T D K O Y J Y G X
W W H L E X I K X U G A U P A H X I L J
Z N V G Z O A B N E H H G O C C M X D W
T G C A Z Q U S P Q P D P S Y A C X L V
S H N B A Y I O E H D J C E S L A O P R
X M C K F S F S C H C O V M L E N E D E
```